ARRIVAL PRESS

SOUTHERN ENGLAND RHYTHMS

Edited by

TIM SHARP

First published in Great Britain in 1997 by
ARRIVAL PRESS
1-2 Wainman Road, Woodston,
Peterborough, PE2 7BU
Telephone (01733) 230762

HB ISBN 1 85786 554 5
SB ISBN 1 85786 549 9

FOREWORD

Southern England Rhythms is a collection of poems that give an insight into how local poets feel about the area in which they live. The anthology includes verse about landscape, nature, their community and their way of life in general.

I am sure that you will enjoy reading the expressive talents in *Southern England Rhythms* as much as I did, and savour this poetic tour guide in the comfort of your own surroundings.

Tim Sharp
Editor

Contents

BLIND BOY'S DREAM

1ST PRIZE WINNER

Grandmother, grandmother, why can't I see
said the small infant child
Curled up on her knee
As she thought of an answer
A tear fell from her eyes
And this answer she gave
Unable to lie.

You my dear, sweet child
Have been given the gift of touch
Most have been given this gift
But do not need it so much
A flower, some water, the bark of a tree
'Tis your hands sweet grandchild
With which you can see.

Rosalie Gray

To All Traffic Wardens (Goodwill To All Motorists At Yuletide)

2nd Prize Winner

If you see mummy's car
Parked on a yellow line
Please don't write a ticket
It's not her fault but mine.

Mum's gone to post a letter
To Santa - just for me:
I hope to find a present
Under the Christmas tree.

If mummy has to pay the fine
It would be very sad;
I would have to wait another year
For a present from mum and dad.

So lots of hugs and kisses
Just from me to you:
When I grow up I want to be
A traffic warden - just like you.

And every time that Christmas comes
I'll think back to this day
When mummy parked on a yellow line
And didn't have to pay.

Dennis Beton

A VISITING CARD

2ND PRIZE WINNER

I felt a chill and saw at early dawn
a visitor had left his card last night.
Upon the leafless boughs and on the ground
nature had laid a carpet of pure white.

The earth outside had lost its softer feel
yet wily squirrels still pursued a plan.
Their food was there but harder now to find.
In hunger, fearless to my gaze they ran.

The fox had left his furtive hiding place
for changing seasons never change his need.
Though nature blessed him with his bushy coat
on days like these how hard for him to feed!

I huddled ever nearer to the fire.
How comfort shields us from the very worst,
for those who have will never count the cost.
Will never hunger and will never thirst.

I see through warm lit room this wintry scene,
illuminated as a Christmas card.
How easy to survive its harmless touch.
How easy to dismiss and disregard!

I see the sun peep weakly through the clouds
and though still fragile lends its awesome power.
I watch as winter's chill is moistening
and buds peep through with promise soon to flower.

The branches shake their winter burdens clear.
The grass reclaims its purest shade of green.
On frail crystal wings you briefly came
but now, what sign that you have ever been?

John Christopher Cole

THE AWAKENING *2ND PRIZE WINNER*

I stand by the hedgerow,
The night lies calm,
Over pathway and furrow,
The quartered moon has gone,
Now - is the silence
That heralds the dawn.

Night thins into misty trails,
as the horizon brightens,
Starlight glimmers and pales,
Heavy eared grass shivers and sways,
and over the horizon gleams
The first bright ray.

Briars, dew drenched, sparkle,
as I hear the click of a beetle,
the rustle of a field mouse,
The music of a cricket's stridulation,
and the wild rose succours
the early humming bee.

Mute, I stand in the earth's awakening,
Then a lark soars
and joyously sings,
an aria for me.

Hilda Groom

I'M STILL NOT FREE *2ND PRIZE WINNER*

The sun is the warmth you enveloped me with
The moon is the light that was dimmed when you left.
The stars make me think of the love in your eyes
Your colourful smile I see in each rainbow - heaven sent.
    I thought that time had released me
    But am I really free?

I hear your voice on each whispering breeze
Each gust of wind brings you so near,
I see your sweet face in each fluffy white cloud,
As raindrops fall I feel them as tears.
    I thought that time had released me
    But I'm still not free.

The snow is the bleakness I feel inside
The ice is the cold window that keeps us apart,
Do you still love me in your new world?
Do you know that you still have my heart?
    I thought that time had released me
    But I know I'm still not free.

The thunder's roar is the sound of my anger
As my once complete life is left unwhole,
The damp grey mist swirls round my body
Like your loving arms around my soul.
    I thought that time had released me
    But I'm not free
    Do I really want to be . . . ?

Zena Rowland

VILLAGES LOST

Our county of Sussex in years gone by
Had villages small that caught the eye
Clusters of cottages, church and green
Ducks on the pond, a pretty scene
Quiet lanes, peace to be found
Trees, hedgerows and fields all around
Along came the planners, builders and all
Now we have nothing but urban sprawl.

Peggy Norrell

ANGELS

Bedpans and drip stands, lined against the wall.
'Sharps' bins and laundry cages, don the polished hall.
Nurses rushing up and down, do work that never ceases.
Checking pulses, wiping brows and blessing all the sneezes.
Beds to make, in pristine shape, in regimental line.
Beeping of the monitors, the cold fans constant whine.
Curtains drawn for privacy, when doctor does his rounds.
Grunts and groans and tiny screams, are ever present sounds.
It takes a special person, to tread the 'medics' path,
knowing when to sympathise, knowing when to laugh.
The struggles made to make the grade are often fraught with pain
Yet nearly all that qualified, would do it all again.
From dawn 'til dusk they soldier on, yet rarely they complain.
With all the trials that face them, they manage to stay sane.
Do they deserve a medal? Oh yes. It's overdue.
And as they take the medal, give them a pay rise too.
We should appreciate their task, and not just when we're ill.
'Cos after all, it's often them that get the bitter pill.

Harriett Dalley

Summer Blackbird

Black of plume, divine in song
   Summer blackbird stay with me
Evening joy to hear always
   Yet winter comes and joy is gone.
Shadows now and you and I
   Meet on chilled garden earth,
Mourn together summer's gone
   But brightly shines your golden eye;
Mute your voice in dark December
   Yet sleeps there in the earth below
Seeds of summer, joy and song -
   Remember, O remember.

Michael Rowson

In My Head

In my head I feel like a bomb has just hit me.
In my head a sort of ghost keeps on bugging me
I get scared in my head . . .
When I close my eyes I see someone,
in my head; someone is saying to me
I'm getting a BMX . . .

In my head I keep thinking there is someone watching me,
in the curtains. In my head I keep thinking
that my friends might stop liking me.
Above my head, I think there is a spider looking at me
and crawling around.

Maybe I should stop watching horror stories.

Maria Holmes (12)

Life Is An Open Book

Oh! The graceful butterfly
alighting on my open book.
Flexing fragile wings, oh, my!
Entranced, I look and look.

I think how wondrous life would be
if I were a butterfly.
Drifting high and flying free.
But I'm just me, oh, (sigh)!

Suddenly my mother's *tut* -
'Hey! Time to wash the dishes'.
Annoyed, I slam the book quite shut.
How fickle is life's wishes.

Brian Humphreys

Ode To Sussex

Across the downs from Chichester to Kent,
Along the shore, this side of Portsmouth and the Isle of Wight;
I think of you and smile and pause awhile.
You are my anchor, you have been my friend,
You've listened to me when I cried with pain,
And given me comfort from your highest brow
With views that stay forever in my brain.
The one track, past times railway line
That winds and turns through fields of golden grain.
The memories of first loves and the kiss.
Of nuts and bluebells gathered in the mists;
Fresh mushrooms cooked for breakfast,
And the smell. I've loved you well.
Through woods and villages that lead to Selsey Bill.
. . . I love you still . . .

Jill Harding

Waiting

Silver chromed chairs once a trendy fashion.
Efficient receptionists, brisk and stern.
'Mrs Hall, is your hearing aid switched on?
Well you had better or you'll miss your turn'.
Screaming kids, mums stressed out, all patience gone.
'Dr Clarke's running late, helping to teach
the new doctor today'. The old man waits.
The cancer, tasting triumph, also waits.

Joy Aldridge

Pilchards And Cream

With pasties and pilchards and mackerel and crabs,
Cream scones and lardy cake, saffron and dabs.
Hog's pudd'en and lobsters and strawberries and cream,
All go to make Cornwall a gastronome's dream.

The seagulls are 'ansome, but beware of that 'splat'
When they hover and soar - oops! Was that your best hat?
And if you eat alfresco, you'd better watch out,
For they'll steal that crab sandwich from under your snout.

Their staple diet nowadays must be fish and chips,
For they'll snatch it away a'fore it reaches your lips.
There's mussels and limpets, stuck fast to the rocks,
Cider and mead, and of course, Cripplecock's.

Cornish fudge, Cornish farings and sweet Cornish honey,
Whether clover or heather, be it set hard, or runny,
I've travelled old England, north, south, east and west,
But I love dear old Cornwall - it's simply the best.

Hilda Jones

UNTITLED

I wonder what it feels like
To know that today you will die.
I wonder how many could take it
Who'd collapse, break down and cry.

I wonder what it feels like
To know that you've been betrayed
By someone you cared for and trusted,
Who's now helping you to your grave.

I wonder what it feels like
To have nails through your hands and your feet,
And blood dripping down from a prickly crown
On a body that's battered and beat.

I wonder what it felt like
As He called out to the One in the sky,
And the crowd gathered round as the gentle young man
Was cut down from His cross on high.

I wonder what would happen
If Jesus came back today,
I wonder if we us Christians
Would treat Him in just the same way?

Patricia Dyer

ROSE

She was failing forties fast
With red petals in her hair.
Her finger ring roots were rough,
Though her eyes shined just as rare.
Her mouth was filled with thorns
And her tongue one red ripped bulb,
But her voice was still as soft
As virgin snow on the first winter's cold.

Now my Rose stumbles when she walks
Though dignity keeps her chin high.
My Rose I watched you and I wished
I could kiss you when you cry.
I wish I could have planted you years ago
And watch you as you blossomed and bloomed.
Instead my part is to dig you up and
Lay you to rest in your mother's womb.

Matthew Friday

Lake Windermere's Open Heart

In seconds on some cosmic clock
Beauty bloomed from ravished rock.
Hills became miracles in time
Then matured into majesty sublime.
Soon colonies such as the conifer
Did dignity over nakedness confer.

Morning mists capping countless hills
Condense, feeding tiny roots from rills,
Then trickle down towards verdant vales,
Like God's constancy which never fails,
Making lovely lake-land waters clear,
Which refresh everything living near.

Pines, reaching for their share of sky,
Growing green, strong, straight and so high
With their saw toothed fern-like tops,
Form feather edges where earthiness stops
And far starlit strands of space start,
Framing Windermere's open heart.

Ronald Rodger Caseby

SHOPPING

There was a time when shopping was not a problem at all
I reached the top and lower shelves with ease, because I'm tall.
But, oh, I do have such a job since my poor back got sore,
to reach down to the lower shelves, they're nearly on the floor!

Then, one bright summer morning, a trolley parked near mine.
A man about my age and height looked up to the top shelf and sighed.
I've noticed since I'm getting older these top shelves are higher, I fear.
Because of my arthritic shoulder, my rice pudding I cannot get near.

I smiled sweetly and said, 'Sigh no more, my good man,
I will get you your pudding at once,
So if you want any, just tell me how many?',
then suddenly I saw my chance.

Well he was most grateful and awfully nice and said,
'Madam, if by any chance there is anything I could do
while I'm here, so to speak, for you?'

I said, 'Yes, oh there is. You see it's like this,
my back is in trouble, I cannot bend double,
and my seedless raisins I miss'.

And now this kind friend, knowing I cannot bend
and I am aware of his limits,
He bends down for the peaches, I reach up for the cream,
as shoppers we now make the perfect team.
We can do it in just twenty minutes!

So, we worked out a rota and we each got our quota.
We're now using just the one trolley,
as shopping for one really isn't much fun,
tea for two is a great deal more jolly.

So, in spite of our vision, which is partial, I fear,
and the problems that brings can cause chagrin,
But with sight far or near, it was perfectly clear,
that we both had an eye for a bargain.

Trudy Keijzer

Memories

In the corner of an attic,
There sits an old bear,
Amongst boxes of junk,
Who knows he is there?

His balding fur, and only one eye
Stares out, across the room,
But in his mind's eye,
He sees beyond the gloom.

Warm sun on his face,
The sweet smell of grass,
He hears laughter of children,
How quick time does pass!

How grand he once looked,
All plumped full of sawdust,
With his shiny button eyes,
And the red bow was a must.

But what memories he has,
Spends the hours quietly whiling,
Though take time to look,
And you'll see he is smiling!

Kerri Fordham

ODE TO THE FARMERS

Plough ye well, 'til earth be tilled,
Then plant some seed, for good crops.
Farmers barn, with hay is filled,
For soon enough, the winter drops.
Toil thee well, 'tis timely gone,
Sweat of thy brow, earns a crust.
All good growth, and reward won.
Pray to the Lord, in Him we trust.
Shire's will pull, through the mud,
Plough's going steady, leaving a rut.
All is made with sweat and blood,
Blisters on hands, and many a cut.
At close of day, when sun is low,
Farmers, and horses, lay to rest.
They be up at dawn, to reap, and sow,
For the farmers, by God, are truly blessed.

Thomas Bicknell

BYPASSED BEAUTY

Have you ever watched a seagull, its body gleaming white
Against a stormy, purple sky, perform its graceful flight?
Have you ever seen a wave rise from the ocean green and dark
And curl itself into a lovely iridescent arc?
Have you ever, in the evening when the sun begins to sink,
Watched the heavens change from blue and grey to turquoise, gold
and pink?
Have you ever passed a garden and been suddenly aware
Of the scent of honeysuckle all around you in the air?
Have you stood upon the Sussex Downs, surveyed the empty scene,
And then noticed red roofs nestling in a hollow in the green?
Have you ever thought that in the rush some other place to be
We miss such a lot of beauty as we look but seldom see?

Doris Rhodes

MY BURDEN

The music of paradise,
Singing of the living,
What claim have I,
Temper with no compassion,
But I've got my pride,
My pillow, a doorstep,
The singing, remembrance of lullabies,
There's pain in the darkness,
It's not pity wanted,
My pride comes with the night,
But the daylight makes me prideless,
I did have class,
Enjoy paradise - only contempt,
Conform to life - no comment.

J McAllister

WINTER

Winter is here, we're caught in its clasp
The autumn has gone - escaped at last
But listen the birds they sing their chorus
Spring is nigh - it's nearly upon us
They've laid their eggs, their young to hatch
Spring has last year's colours to match
I've planted my seeds - have you done yours?
To gaze on my garden - the neighbours applause
My baskets and pots a dream to behold
How much did they cost - they'll never be told
The sun will shine and so will I
Winter will pass by and by
So come on spring - my garden awaits
To compete with the neighbours
I mustn't be late.

J Follett

MILLENNIUM

Two thousand years since Christ was born
And counting years AD began
And man received a further chance,
To save himself from evil's choice
As in the Book of Revelations about the first millennium,
There Satan was chained up for a thousand years to come
And when this time was over his chains and ties he broke,
And scattered discontentment at just one evil stroke.
In the last millennium, world wars, anguish and strife,
Have shown the devil's freedom to cause hatred in this life.

Man has made much advancement in this last millennium
The car, train, plane and rocket, and alas the atom bomb.
The towns, the cities, man has built, his travel to the moon.
What will the next millennium hold,
Where will the next move be?
This time there's been the sailing boat and liners on the sea.

Man has extracted oil wells and invented CFC's,
He near destroyed the planet through the damage this has caused,
With the ozone thinning over us,
The greenhouse effect, with adverse radiation, our protection to
neglect.
Man learned to split the atom and harness it for power,
Until there was a disaster, and man died hour after hour.

Man cut down the rain forests in effect we have shrunk the world,
Oh what will the new millennium hold, an age of heat, and age of cold?
Will man live longer to enjoy this earth,
Will disease be beaten and we enjoy good health,
Will love be conquering and abolish hate,
Will peace break out and wars be gone,
Will dove with olive branch return,
And peace reign in the new millennium?

Janet McKinney

Water Pictures

Water, water, gently plopping,
Relaxing, soothing, tensions stopping -
Falling into garden pool,
Swirling, bubbling, sounding cool.

Mountain streams flow swiftly by -
Falling crystal clear o'er cliffs so high,
Into pools where chill mists cling
To trees and bushes where warblers sing.

In forest glades, see the peaty pools
Reflecting trees and stars like jewels -
A murmuring brook twists slowly by,
Brushing the banks with barely a sigh.

A turgid canal with barges bright,
There's hardly a movement 'til the locks are in sight.
On the banks sit the fishermen winding reels -
What do they catch? Just loads of eels.

Walk by the river, watch the flow -
Cows in the shallows where the water's low.
There's two boats in midstream - racing, no doubt -
Both teams pull strongly at the cox's shout.

We've water all round, it's part of the scene -
We need it for pleasure, and it keeps Britain green.
Conserve it we must - waste not a drop,
It's raining again, will it never stop?

Mae Smith

The Country Walk

Walking across the Sussex downs
They are all covered in autumn browns
Trees stand there stripped and bare
The have a beauty beyond compare.

Most of the animals are hiding away
Awaiting a springtime day
They are all huddled safe and warm
Protected from the winter storm.

As I walk down the lane
I remember once again
Of days with my mother
Of how we would love to walk with each other.

Sandra Lunnon

A Piece Of My Heart

I love you in so many ways,
The way you talk, laugh and smile,
I wish we were on holiday next to the River Nile,
When I look at you, I find myself decay,
By the way, I wish I could reach out and touch you,
I'll never understand why the girls around you,
Feel the same way, like I do, for you too,
My love for you will grow, too.
I love the way you act,
The way you stand, the way you shake hands,
I wish we were listening to our favourite bands,
You are always full of your wonderful tact,
The wonderful thing I love best of all,
Is because you are you!

Delphine Simmons (15)

SUSSEX COUNTRYSIDE

For those of us who here
Reside, we love our Sussex
Countryside.
The wide sweep of the
Downland hills, the folds and
Valleys neatly tilled, with
Sheep which graze upon
The grass, such peace, what
More can we ask.
The trees of beauty size and
Shape with us thoughts of
God awake.

The bluebell's carpet woods
And lane, to tell us
Spring is here again.
Summer's bees that sleepy
Drone over garden's haze
Of home.
Autumn's glint, the far seas
Shine, from the Downs the
View is mine, laid below
Like jewelled crowns from
The splendid Sussex
Downs.

Kim Trask

THE TAY BRIDGE DISASTER

Bridge
moaning
under load
stress, strain, shear, creep.
Keep
safe,
structure!
Strut, tie, rod,
frame, lattice beam
hold!
Load
too high -
Joints yield force -
design error
fails
bridge.
Terror,
collapsing
lattice girders:
Death!

Gerhard Both

THE WHITE HORSE

I saw it gallop by in a flash of white,
It looked so magical in the pitch black night.
The horse roamed wild and free
No-one saw him, but me
He was gone as fast as he had come
To gallop the hillside once again
He looked so beautiful he looked so strong.
But he was gone before too long . . .

Julia Welland (12)

Duty Free

I'll be in the States next week, you said,
And my heart gave a lurch at the thought
Of your duty free gifts that would give
me a lift, as you lied as I cried as
we fought.

Next time you go, say a big hello from a
gift-wrapped wife who cries. And say if
you will, I wish her no ill.
I merely hope she *dies*.

Barbara Cumming

Watching Life Go By!

Small Chinese man in grey trilby hat,
Stops on the corner to chat about this and that.
Looks very smart in his flannels and jacket.
Wonder they can talk above all the traffic!
Lots of hand gestures from the Chinese man
Stiff upper lip from the one of our clan.
Sunny day, people walking dogs on leads
And carrying shopping.
Traffic constant, all sorts of noise
Large lorries, horns blaring
Ugly signs of people swearing.
Radio in the house nearby blasting,
While the decorators are plastering.
Youths are jogging,
One old lady coughing.
Husbands coming to the car at last
This just looks like a stage show
And these are the cast.

Lyn Roberts

TREES

If there were no trees upon our land,
How bleak our lives would be.
No leafy boughs, no birds to sing,
No towering majesty.

No seasons change for us to see
As winter fades away.
No springtime buds upon the trees
From April into May.

No summertime, when trees are dressed
In all their shades of green,
The mountain ash, the silver birch,
The willow by the stream.

No autumn colours should we see
If trees were not around.
No autumn tints of fallen leaves
As they lay on the ground.

Be thankful that the trees are here,
And do your best to see,
That millions can enjoy them still
For all eternity.

Joan Kilby

JOBS FOR THE BOYS!

In line with my colleagues I'm forced to complain;
These working conditions are really a strain,
I've been asked by my comrades to make this request;
That you treat them all fairly, each one like the rest.

The post needed filling, of that we are sure,
And in time of recession we need all the more
To employ someone of adequate skill,
Who's qualified greater than 'run of the mill'.

I tell you, this job's quite a challenge for me,
Running a branch of this big company,
Because it's the first job that I've ever had,
So I hope I'll do well and be just like you, dad.

Dawn Mitchell

Winter In Waiting

Remember a day in October, when we ran
hand in hand across golden stubble,
and corn stalks scratched our bare legs?
Darkly in the orchard,
horses tossed away the last of the summer flies
and idly swished their tails
as pale evening light drained into the horizon.
Only we knew why we ran panting into the lane,
stopping no more than a couple of times to catch our breath.
Ours was a secret race against time and a longing for a new season.

With great good humour barns were replete and brimming with grain.
Apples gleamed, spaced side by side in the store,
home-made preserves stowed away on the larder shelf -
            red, orange and purple -
waited to be spread on hot buttered toast.
Hasten, hasten, whispered our feet on the first fallen leaves.
Several half-open conkers had dropped to the ground
            and lay grinning by the door.
We settled into deep-cushioned chairs with contentment
and even as summer sorcery ebbed away into the enchantment of
            autumn,
we knew that when winter breathed
the first breaths of frost and snow on the bitter air
the country side would be ready and waiting.

Rosa Johnson

An Ode To Save Hindhead Common

Oh please do something, and make it soon,
Don't wait until we're living on the moon.
Hindhead would lose such splendid views
Unless you bring us some good news.

Queues of traffic daily, always round the bend,
Or, to avoid these, our country lanes they wend.
Which disturbs all our local villages
And, also, upsets their peaceful images.

You'll upset all our wildlife -
Even the insects that are rife.
Perhaps, new homes they'll never find,
Are you sure you would not mind?

The heather - such a lovely sight,
For the bees to use for their delight.
Even the honey - you will I'm sure agree
Is so natural, and tastes heavenly.

And don't forget all the birds,
Don't let's keep exchanging words.
Their song would leave this idyllic scene,
If you move their trees - now so green.

They will be there forever more,
If only a tunnel you will bore.
So! Let's get this important tunnel on its way,
And, please! Please! Don't delay.

Pam Bryder

The Word Stranger

away from the hullabaloo
dusty, crusty, solitary on a musty shelf
sat the stranger by himself
chomping on a golden loaf
crumbs of words dropping to the ground
would surround the pedantic peasants
who skulked around
fighting for leftovers -
all that might be found:
a 'sangfroid' a 'salubrious salmagundi salsify',
a 'mellifluous memorandum of meiosis',
the prognosis, they say, is dim,
clarity, charity, for their own sanity
simplicity sacrificed is ill advised
wipe the intellectualism from those eyes
pale! pail! Death draws near -
and the colossus dictionary of imbued fear!
- contained within a
single
autonomous academic sphere,
where stood the masked stranger
ignorant of everything
except the word and
fear of intellectual ignorance
as dawn draws near . . .

Roman C McKnell

Life In Frames

Pictures in a house, along the walls
Tell the character, memory recalls.

A time in life, a specific hour,
A history complete, strength and power.

An oil painting of a black horse,
Painted in numbers short and coarse,
Painted by the hand of a child,
Immaturity beguiled.

A Constable scene, no not real,
A fake, but love is its seal.
A gift to someone to show feelings true,
Affection so deep that was always due.

Chinese carved pictures of houses and trees,
That were bought abroad across the seas.
An oriental island for military service,
A time to remember, not to miss.

A large oil painting by an adult hand,
Hangs over the mantelpiece so grand.
A watermill and stream so real,
Life is present to touch and feel.

History and character, stories are told
In pictures, paintings, new and old.

Remove these from a home and this is gone,
The walls are just walls all alone.

Lee Brewin

OUR DAILY WALK AT BEMBRIDGE BAY

A thick frost lay upon the ground this morning when I woke.
And when outside my breath could see, with every word I spoke.
The fences glistened white as white, and all along the gate.
The car went straight away, that's good, to beach, my dogs can't wait.

The wind had dropped along the shore, and though the tide was high.
We walked along the golden sands, my eager dogs and I.
We strolled along the wooded path, amongst the trees, now bare.
And gazed across the rolling waves, a moment without care.

We now head back for home once more, across the pebbles high.
But not a drop of sun could shine, from pale and cloudy sky.
Across the sand dunes, fresh sea breeze, that coldly touched my face.
And morning sounds begin to stir, the wakening human race.

Around the corner, across desolate sand, there is a small cafe.
In summer high, there's no spot spare, in this sheltered little bay.
The dogs, both happy scratch the sand, still ready for a game.
But we climb in car reluctantly; and drive back home again.

Fran Rapley

TODAY'S CHILDREN ARE TOMORROW'S WORLD

There are poor little children in this world, who have the right to live,
They have illnesses that can be cured, if people would only give.
Bone marrow transplants they can have, that is easily done,
They want the money to do the tests - a really big cash sum.

A lot of the money is being spent, -some of us may hear,
A football pitch, an opera house, perhaps a seaside pier.
Give your money to a worthy cause and give these kids a chance,
Forget the lottery, make them smile, let these children dance.

Joyce Ayland

THE GIRL FROM CARDBOARD CITY

dear mum and dad - by telepathic e-mail
e for empathy, ether, extrasensory
maybe on the frequency of a honeybird's wing
or May-bloom petals floating on the breeze
or the distant music of the galaxies

an apology from your Dresden-dolly daughter
your little showpiece, treasure, priceless jewel
who found your coronet of love too big, too heavy
jumped down from the mantelpiece where you liked to keep her
ran for shelter, found it in this cold shop doorway

your love-bird trapped in a cage, taught to talk, perform
could not endure the my's as if you owned her
my girl, my daughter, my car, my prized possession
the weight of chains forged by your expectations
you didn't hear her scream, clenched fists, into her pillow

I couldn't ride the surf of your affection
it broke over me, left me bruised and crushed
I needed air, get my head above the flood tide
here love's tsunami falls back from the shore
of my safe atoll of freedom to be me

bitter-sweet the taste of tears of freedom
sorry and thanks, don't worry, no turning back
dustbins, a blanket, wash in the dew in the park
the wind in my face, the sound of raindrops dancing.
Miss the cat on my bed, the only person I could talk to.

F Diment

SOMERSET STORIES

Somerset whose name derives from summerland of yore,
whose towns and villages encompass legends and folklore,
whose past embraces tales historical and mystic
and figures medieval, modern and majestic.
King Arthur, Guinevere and the knights of the round table,
Sir Galahad and Lancelot - reality or fable?

At Glastonbury, so 'tis said, they sought the Holy Grail,
brought from the Holy Land by Joseph, and thereby hangs a tale,
wherein upon a local hill adjacent to the Tor
he tired, and for support leaned on the staff he bore,
it forthwith blossomed and upon its stem was born
the flower to originate the Glastonbury thorn.

Exmoor is a land of beauty but of mystery and moods,
and a history of intrigue, of fantasies and feuds,
of outlaw groups of which the Doone family was one,
but those who live may also die by bullet and the gun.
Lorna, object of much domestic jealousy, so 'tis said
shot, standing at the altar, whilst waiting to be wed.

Though *Sedgemoor* differs greatly in both nature and terrain,
in terms of tragedy and treachery similarities remain.
Sedgemoor levels is a region, low lying, flood-ridden and flat,
it products peat, as fuel and fertiliser, and willow for the bat.
King Alfred here took refuge as from the battlefield he fled
and allowed a peasant's cakes to burn, for which she boxed his head.

In some caves beneath the Mendips the witch of Wookey can be
found,
who for her sorcerous evil ways against lovers was renowned.
She steadfastly refused for spells and curses to stone
and so some sprinkled holy water from a monk turned her to stone.
Such tales as these are woven into the fabric of our history
but whether fact or fantasy should best, perhaps, remain a mystery.

Lionel Burton

Can It Be

What has happened to England's green and pleasant lands
Its lush green fields and golden sands
Where children could walk with laughter and bliss
And lovers could stroll and share a kiss.

What now we ask, what do we do
Families together are very few
Children roam the streets alone by night
Homeless people are a regular sight

Just take this world and shake it well
You never know and who can tell
In its making it might just have happened
That this world of ours got misshapened

Maybe if it's taken into hand
People might once again understand
That it takes love and sharing to make it whole
Once again maybe our world will have a soul

So please take heart, make a new start
Make a new world, make a new year
Where a child can walk without any fear.

Brenda Moore

A Thought For Easter - Through The Eyes Of A Donkey

Once tied against the door I'd waited in the burning heat;
'Ere long I found the crowd spread cloaks and palms beneath my feet.
The master needed me; though I be just a humble thing,
I was not too lowly on this earth to serve the heavenly King.

With careful tread I picked my way along the palm strewn track,
With joy and pride I felt the weight of Jesus on my back.
On either side I heard the crowd their loud hosannas sing
To praise the gentle carpenter, who was their heavenly King.

The weight upon the dear Lord's back by sinful man was made,
And by His death upon the cross, the awesome debt was paid.
So now this Eastertide again your loud hosannas sing
To praise the Lord, who died for all; your everlasting King.

Margaret Collins

All The World Without

All day the gusty north wind bore
the loosening paint.
Shut in from all the world without
I sat
Content to let the north wind roar
against pane and door.
The fire's red coal rolled,
Beams shook,
The great throat of the chimney
Laughed, while there was no
welcome sound of toil or mirth,
The dog on his paws outspread
Laid to the fire his drowsy head,
A mug of tea simmered on the
fire's hearth, and, close at hand
a poem yet complete.
All day the north wind bore
the loosening paint.
Shut in from all the world without
I sat.
Content.

John Thomas Jones

A Winter's Day

Pebbles collide beneath my feet
As I walk along this rocky street
Cold salt water sprays my face
White horses jump without any grace
The wind is strong the waves get higher
The sun has gone like a forgotten Messiah
The summer seems so far away
There's no sand castles here today
A demanding presence in the form of rain
Rears its beautiful head again
A twisted view to those that scheme
With holiday brochures at every seam
Today is nothing and everything too
As I tiptoe along with hands of blue
A feeling inside is satisfied here
Like an alcoholic in a sea of beer.

David Golden

The Un-Named Traveller

He be a simple man, with simple thoughts and simple ways;
He be of simple means, yet he be not left wanting.
No man be his master, he be no man's slave;
Yet he do be troubled certain, for he be at the cross-roads of life.

Wither he do go for'ard;
Or side away one way, or side away t' other way.
Weary he do be in mind an' body, lay he down upon the sod, t' rest awhile;
The thoughts of travelled ways gone by, of golden morn to wend his way ahead.
'Tis too late, oh! Ye un-named traveller;
For ye be, as mutton be, . . . dead.

Ray Casey

Sussex Chimes

Hamlet never could decide
Which side of heaven to abide
But had he seen the lovely sight
Of Sussex bathed in summer light
Surely then he would have known
That death was something to postpone
Until the creaking hands of winter
Made the oak trees frown and splinter
For in the land of Kipling's prose
In amongst the hand cared roses
And the ancient parish churches
Lies the land of silver birches
Oh let there never be a time
When bells in Sussex cease to chime.

Graham Pidgeon

Epitaph For A Swan

For many years I've wandered by these tranquil lakes
And wondered at the snow-white dignity of cob and pen.

Gliding along in silent majesty,
Feeding from friendly, human hands, and then
Producing cygnets for us all to share.
Grey fluffy things, that grow to be as fair
As they themselves.

No more will this pair breed, and fill our lives with joy,
No more will they swim side by side, and wait
For food, serenely, at the waterside.

Only the pen remains, lost and bewildered, in her lonely state,
Bereft forever, of her faithful mate.

A Dyson

A MOVING EXPERIENCE

My latest move I shan't forget
It's been my most traumatic yet
The loneliest time I've ever known
As I sat listening for the phone
And waited for the words to say
You'll very soon be on your way
With contracts signed and then exchanged
Removal date and time arranged
With boxes to my left and right
I've sat and pondered day and night
And when at last I went to bed
I hoped that I may wake up dead
Instead of which each morn at five
I found that I was still alive
Where ere I go and come what may
That is where I hope to stay.

Dorothy Everett

DYSLEXIC POET

Poems animals inside my head, who will kill themselves, if they
can't break free.
Roaming across the page, making nests on the lines.
Eating each other, only the strong will survive.
Lords of the jungle in print, roaring defiantly.
Words soar eagle like, swimming pike jaws, the biting remark.
Out of the dark comes mole, not secretive badger me.

Kevin Turner

The Sunset

Cruising along the darkening skyline,
The crimson glow of the setting sun
Sends a promise of a bright tomorrow,
Leaving the dissolving blueness of the day
To be pierced by celestial lights.

Wrapped in the shades of nearby shapes,
Our arms entwined, we watch with awe
The fading scene of a glorious day.
Across the fields the distant glare
Of cars, of pubs, of hotel lights
Reveal man's ever frantic quest
To meet demands for his delights,
While nature sinks to rest.

Brenda Wilson

Lottery Dreams

I have this dream
Of a lovely country cottage
Just enough for one
Where I can laze away the hours
Smell the flowers, feel the sun,
Hear the birds singing
See butterflies winging,
Be at peace with the world
When the day is done,
But it's only a dream,
That I know can never be,
Although things will be different
If I win that lottery!

V Pearse

GODS, FAITHS AND MAN

Many Gods and faiths have come and gone
invented by Egyptian, Roman, Greek
who served them and then let them fade away
to make way for some different deity.

Of those extant Christ's teachings seem to give
a gentle basis by which man may live
with others of his species in the world.
It is a simple faith which, kept intact
and unelaborated by *man's* rules
will cause no harm and might just do some good.

The trouble lies with man whose arrogance
leads him to interfere with what he finds
and take the bits he likes, and form in sects.
Each sect becomes intolerant and then
the burnings start, the holy wars, crusades,
man's inhumanity to man and holocausts.

So let us all rejoice for common prayer
or Holy Mass, or call it what you will,
it keeps the faith alive and strengthens souls
who otherwise might falter on the way.

But don't let any sect become too strong
or so convinced that it alone is right,
there's danger in apostles, unrestrained,
(they don't have a monopoly of light).

Some people think scientifically and say;
'Can one believe man really rates a God?'
A single species, homo sapiens,
is nothing when one thinks in cosmic terms?

The choice which faces one seems bleak;
is it faith or evidence you seek?

James Franks

TREASURED BY OUR FAMILY

James Benjamin McAvoy was his name
He had a little bit of fame
A royal navy man was he
spent his life roaming the sea
His journal started 1859
Is here with me it is now mine
I am his great granddaughter a housewife
Reading all about his life
Writings tell of far off places
Different accents foreign faces
When on leave his interests were many
Heard Spurgeon preach did he give a penny
Visited theatres and music halls
attended soirees and a few balls
Thoughts of a quiet dinner with an interesting lady
Seeing his sister's adorable baby
Wondering if a certain lady would welcome his kisses
But she wasn't destined to be his missus
Mentioned one Captain Thrupp a friend called Harris
Visiting the Lees at Greenwich Palace
He was shipwrecked on his way to Australia
I wonder did he feel a failure
His death was unexpected poisoned food
A last diary entry he was in a low mood
Where is his grave so far away
I would love to go and say
A whispered thank you for the journal left to me
It's treasured by our family.

Maurine Clensy Smith

LEARNING LINES

Let's dream an ocean
where we all are
playing Frisbee until dusk
the only anger being the fire
in our frivolous hearts

each satisfied with what we do
each savouring the soothing dew

Like lions in a tall cage
we look skyward
for Venus to wink approval
and shed a showering heavy rain
to cleanse our dry hair

we in our safety a populous stew
not a captain but a loyal crew

Pens are our coarse coral
under our tiptoes
words only waves of endeavour
that sprinkle ideas onto our skin
like a liquid pollen

while we this dream intend to pursue
in no rush to form a linked queue

So when it rains tell me
to slowly wake up
and remember each instance
so in the fresh day's battering blue
I have no need for a worn out autocue.

Andy McPheat

The Promise Of Spring

The snow is here it's winter,
Flakes fall softly down,
Fluttering past the window
Just like thistle down.
Covering the ground
With a carpet white.
It truly is a wonderful sight.

No flowers, or birds meet our gaze,
They snuggle all together,
Away from snow and wind storms,
And the winter weather,
The river is frozen, the sky is grey,
But our hearts are warm within,
Because we know that soon will come
That wonderful glorious spring.

Nancy Scott

Mickael

I have a brother called Mickael by name boy is he one big
pain.
In the morning when I need a wash he's in there first oh my
gosh.
I wait and wait while minutes go by, by the time he finishes
it's time to fly.
He comes out smiling without a care of how long he was in
there but my brother whatever he does I will always love
him even if he takes ages to wash.

Reanne Graefe

No

The little word that's hard to say,
Folk fail to use it every day;
From mums and dads with children small,
To those retired and not on call.

In bygone days a glance, a stare,
No need for anyone to blare;
The young were seen but were not heard,
Some thought their views were just absurd.

It's good that thoughts and views now share,
It's good when parents show true care;
But times arise both night and day,
When parents should the word *no* say.

Those parents with their children young,
Those older folk with life's work done;
When folk come begging with tales of woe,
There are those times you should say *no*.

If there is a task to do,
Make sure it is not always you;
Others sometimes want to go,
Their only chance if you say *no*.

John Paulley

Bird's Song

Awake to dawn chorus
a beautiful sound
from birds up in trees
and some on the ground.
It makes me feel happy
that spring will appear
what a shame we can't hear this
throughout all the year.

Relaxing spring evening
go outside to hear
a beautiful song
so special and clear
I wish I could catch it
and lock it in time
the song of the blackbird
singing its rhyme.

J James

YOURS FOREVER

(After the Bomb)

As we lay here,
falling out around us
I remember the days we've shared
thoughts that my mind has spared,
for days like these.

As we face this
let us never forget
the pact we made
that tomorrow would never come,
as it doesn't for some.

Now it is all over,
the pain has gone away
nothing can harm you now.

Now it is all over,
my pain has just begun,
I will have to wait
I will see you soon
I will never leave you again.

Gavin Sheffield

A Kentish Lament

There's Meg; she spends her pounds on booze,
Kyle, he feels happy; no matter what he'll lose,
Both shop for fags at Strood's Terrace Store.
They have two keys, that fit each other's doors.

Number eight, Terrace Way,
Sees that young couple down 'from Birmingham way',
Kent has always been their home,
Their sour, washed up, sad - they have no real home.

Chatham docks and Medway river,
Medway folk observe then shrug and quiver,
Rochester's closing down its docks,
High street shops close in dismay, at five o'clock.

Hempstead shopping mall; thrives each day,
As local shops are forced to play -
That dirty game of lowering prices,
'til their shops are carved into little slices.

Estates in Maidstone, Tunbridge, Folkestone,
Seem grey, so dull, lacking fire and brimstone,
People pretending to be so brave,
Hopes, forlorn that dishevelled Thanet might be saved.

Mr Jones from number six Terrace Way,
Canvas bag, stick, pipe and his asthma spray.
Walks down to his prized small, garden plot,
Where he's punched in the face by some fifteen year old clot.

Rapists in parks, stabbings in streets,
Kent, today is for many so bleak,
People don't talk of life like they did,
Englishmen tend to live, under tight lids.

Owen Roberts

A Dream

Yesterday was but a while ago
Our childhood quickly passed - and yet I know
That a dream had formed, and there was started
And through many a long year it has still lasted.

In streets we played - high walls around
And brick upon brick houses there abounded,
We played around the streets - oh so bare
No greenery - no trees were there.

'When we grow up' - thus we talked and dreamed
Of living in a green green land,
Where we could see the setting sun
Settle, nestling softly o'er on the horizon.

See the skyline ablaze with glory
Would this dream come true? Or just be a fairy story?
Then one day - oh joy - it happened!
Our dream house came - and there was fashioned
An area so bright - so clean -
Our very own - our village green!

Our children played and grew up bonny
Though there were times when we had little money,
These were happier days, they had the green - the air - the sun
Saw the wonder in the sky when day was done.

We were content
Our dream came true
Our home - our children
And the green to view

M Martin

MILLENNIAL SONG

Nigh two thousand years ago
(Is the tick of time so slow?)
Near two thousand miles away
(How far glows the dawn of day?)
God came down to planet earth
(Mary gave Him human birth).

What is that to you and me?
Third millennium people, we -
Long ago and far away -
We must live our lives today,
Interface via Internet,
Surf the Web - and yet - and yet -

What defines reality?
Where is our morality?
What is goodness? Where is truth?
Why does beauty die with youth?
Questions, puzzles - then death's night
Snuffs out life's uncertain light.

Gurus, mantras, horoscopes,
New age system's mock our hopes;
Yet our questions are not stilled -
Deep needs cry to be fulfilled.
Money, power, success and fame -
Are these all? - Life but a game?

Brilliant thinkers spend their days
Groping in the moral maze;
But by coming here to earth
God makes clear His view of worth -
Jesus is His way, His life
The truth to answer all our strife.

David Gurney

MURUROA

You really don't know how sorry we feel,
That we have to come in our ships of steel.
You realise of course we've come
Just to explode our little bombs.
You needn't feel the least bit fearful,
We'll be so very, very, careful.
We really must check that this device,
Will behave properly. Please eat your rice.
We are French, we know our right.
If you resist, you'll have to fight.
But really, look, you must be fair.
We'll only radiate your air,
And make a little, little pouf.
You needn't get in such a huff.
There is no need for anger or grief.
We're only making little holes in your reef.

S Fortt Gill

NORTHWOOD HILL

The dog rose leads me, as it did before
- down pathways brimming with the growth of June . . .
Bracken, and tall nettles deep
- and bird-song filling all the glade asleep . . .
and riotous campion festooned
            with cuckoo-spit

What happened to the years between?
. . .it seems one summer, and they all have gone
through the treacherous tunnel that we once called 'time' . . .
And yet the joyous dog rose leads me on.

Gill Gordon

THE PASSING OF TIME

Crammed into a small church,
on the outskirts of our town,
Filled to overflowing,
To say goodbye to a friend.

The woman vicar read aloud,
The story of his life,
I never knew he achieved so much,
For he was too modest to tell.

I tried to stop my tears,
But I was never strong enough,
The sound of Belinda Carlisle filled the church,
Singing 'Heaven is a place on earth'.

John and I, helped carry the coffin,
To his final resting place,
And almost two years later,
The events are as clear as the day.

Thank God he had the strength,
To truly believe in God above,
Never once doubting His word,
Never ever questioning why.

Martin McGregor

UNTITLED

I am rough,
I am tough,
I am strong but thick
Like two bricks I pick on
all the smaller kids,
We put them in the bins
and slam down the lids
on those silly little puny kids.

I am rough
I am tough
I cough on all the smaller boffs,
I nick their toffs and
give them my smelly socks.

I am rough
I am tough
and I like to bluff
and knock them down
in one big puff.

Deborah Tugwell (10)

SEASONS

Winter has begun to pass
Spring draws nearer every day
Birds have started nesting
Lambs are on the way
The farmers busy planting
Seeds to feed us all
Soon the corn and wheat fields
Will be growing strong and tall
The summer sun and showers
Help fill out the fields
So as autumn starts to follow
It is time to reap the yields
A race against the weather
To beat the wind and rain
But once it is safely gathered
We can face the winter again.

D Hayter

The Old Clickety-Clack

It's not quite the same
When you travel by train,
Now the steamers have gone
From the track,
And continuous rail
On which coaches now sail,
Has subdued the old clickety-clack.

There's not the same thrill
On the long haul uphill,
Now the steamers have gone
From the track,
And that double-tone horn
With its note so forlorn,
Mocks the passing of clickety-clack.

There's nought but a dream
For us lovers of steam,
Now the steamers have gone
From the track,
But on nights clear and fine
By a derelict line,
You may still hear that clickety-clack.

Albert Hart

April

April is a lovely time,
Full of spring flowers.
Warmed by golden sunshine
Cooled by silver showers.
Scarlet tulips proud in the border
Crocus under the tree,
On the hill yellow daffodils
Dancing and tossing free.

Calling birds, cooing doves
Robins whistle shrill.
Sooty blackbirds singing high
Through bright orange bill.
A time of growth and promise,
Of change in many ways,
Exciting and vibrant
Before May's warm sleepy days.

Marge Chamberlain

Changing Times

He was old he was worn
Bewhiskered, dishevelled, so forlorn
Clothes that shared a better day
Shoes had trod a weary way
But his eyes, they sparkled still
Reflecting bright his inner will
Such change these eyes had witnessed so
Now here a friend that was a foe
Where before the shells were aimed
Friends were lost or sometimes maimed
Blood was shed with bayonet steel
No counselling given, no appeal
Tears for loved one who had paid
The ultimate price, do memories fade?
These eyes entranced within a spell
Of dirt, of mud, of instant hell
Time now has changed, that war is done
To shake the hand that held the gun
Each his own loss to call to mind
Forgiveness each his own to find
Absolution then an end endeavour
Forgiveness hopes, forgotten never.

Bill Chase

Fergus The Fox

Fergus the fox was very bright,
Went out hunting every night.
Always back before it got light,
Keeping out of the farmers' sight.

Then one time it all went wrong,
Staying out when the light was strong.
He heard the hounds coming along,
And the huntsmen to whom they belong.

Fergus decided it best to go,
Across the fields but he didn't know.
Whether the hunt was fast or slow,
The hounds and the huntsmen went Tally Ho!

But soon he had a great idea,
Knowing there was a hole quite near.
Dashing in he could still hear,
The hounds and the horsemen giving a cheer.

The dogs ran into the hole in the hill,
Then suddenly heard a very loud shrill.
Frightened they froze and all stood still,
They should have fled but hadn't the will.

All quaking and shaking in total loss,
The miserable pack of canine dross.
One dog screamed who was clearly the boss,
'Run for your lives it's the train from Kings Cross'.

Now Fergus slipped out with a smile on his face,
Trotting back home at an elegant place.
Happy to see the hounds in disgrace,
The huntsmen as well had been put in their place.

James Hime

A Poem

A poem
is a journey through words.
A manifesto
for its purpose,
proposed and composed
in metered, thoughtful
resourceful prose.
A poem is
single,
yet married to many.
Distinct from the poet
the second it's penned.
Meaning, deep, different
its message is dead
until from the drawer
it's explored and read
or said
to an audience of
inquisitive minds, unwrapping
their feelings and
senses not mine.
And sensing the timing
rambling or rhyme,
its literate alliterations
always align.
And so to the poet,
divorced from its subject,
senses new feelings and
moods to convey,
blending suggestions,
concealing connections,
connecting collections,
to collate and array.

T Noel Davies

To My Son

You sometimes read what men have done
And oft times you are told
But I say do it yourself my son
Before you grow too old

I sometimes wish I could take my head
And place it on your own
But you have to struggle yourself instead
And find your way alone

The young can never take just being told
They have to make the grind
I wish they would listen to the old
For the lessons of mankind

One day when you are old my son
I'm sure you will feel like I
I hope you feel what in life you've done
Will never make you sigh

So there you are and I wish you well
In everything that you do
What the years will bring you cannot tell
I am sure you will pull through.

George Dragon

A Politician's Promise

Put a cross next to my name
It'll be something you won't regret,
I'll improve your living standards
And get the country out of debt.

I'll make sure that all the homeless
Are housed and off the street
And I'll bring back law and order
With more bobbies on the beat.

I'll ensure that all our children
Get a first class education
And I'll return this divided isle
Once again into a nation.

All these things I'll do
And much more if you so desire,
Just remember to vote for me
The Right Honourable Billy Liar.

Bob Sharp

THE CHOIR

As I entered the cathedral they started singing,
And I slipped into a side chapel to sit and listen.
The hymn was being sung by sweet young voices,
And the music of the organ filled the air with melody.
The familiar words of praise echoed around the pillars
And eased into my heart with nostalgic memory.

The stone figures lying in the walls
Slept undisturbed by the anthem's vibrant sound.
They had heard for centuries the voice of worship
Raised upwards towards the roof in jubilation,
Only I had forgotten the peace those words could bring,
And I was poorer for the lapse in contemplation.

The service over, the choirboys all departed,
Walking two-by-two down through the central aisle,
The censer swung, and the sweet smoke of the incense
Like a Benediction over my bowed head curled.
I sat a while and listened to the organ
Before I, too, left and went out into the world.

Anita Dye

To A Young Thrush

Short days ago
You didn't know
of any foe!

Here - now you lie.
Cannot reply -
to such as I.

For you to sing -
then, take to wing -
was everything!

Was it this cold?
Our feline, bold -
that one should scold?

Suspicion bring? . . .
Examining . . .
there is nothing! . . .

So young you seem,
though eyes don't gleam.
Your coat, pristine.

Fine, feathered bird,
you never heard,
if something stirred!

Not speak of you -
sweet songster who
sees not my view?

Your endless sleep;
shall doubtless reap;
cause one to weep.

Deep now I place
your form - encase
in earth's embrace.

B Stevens

HUSTLE AND RUSH

Get up in the morning
Get showered and dressed
Oh dear! My skirt's not pressed,
Oh! What a mess.
Get out another,
That's nearly as bad.
It always happens when one stays out late,
Hop into bed, and sleep like a log,
Then upon waking, needing a hair of the dog.
Why am I grouchy?
I'll see him tonight.
Then it'll be the same, tomorrow morning.
I must get up, as soon as it's light,
As I get home too tired,
To prepare my clothes right.
I must look good in my job,
To impress my customers.
Put on my best manners,
It's only right.
If I have no customers,
I may as well give up
There won't be a job to go to.
It's as simple as that . . .

P Wright

SOPHIE GEORGIA

She learns new tricks at a racing pace
In her fluffy white cardy and a blouse of lace
She's my tumble tot terror with an angel's face
Her name is Sophie Georgia.

She laughs and she cries and affection she vies
She can't catch the cat; but God how she tries
My tumble tot terror with the sparkling eyes
My sweetest Sophie Georgia.

She gets all her toys out and stacks them in piles
She points at the pictures we've painted on tiles
A tumble tot terror with the cutest of smiles
My darling Sophie Georgia.

She kisses and cuddles and I love her like mad
She means all the world to me 'cos I am her dad
She's my tumble tot terror and I'll never be sad
Now I've got Sophie Georgia.

Louis Horne

HONEYSUCKLE/WOODBINE

Wild woodbine, olfactory balm,
I love you more since hearing your story;
More tender than the olive or palm
Charmingly fresh with a morning glory.
In France they call you chevre-feuille,
Love child of the body and soul;
The English softly say 'sweet honeysuckle'
Mingling with the notes of the rossingnol;
Emblem of hope and true love,
From the hearts of Tristram and Yseult entwined
You spring to perfume every green grove.

Mary Frances Mooney

A Place I Know

When everywhere is capped with snow
There is a place I know
Where it seems I was meant to be
And as I look around I see
Beauty and bright skies abound
There's also to be found
A friendly and light-hearted atmosphere
Everything seeming into gear
It is along the seashore west
That brings out in you the best

The sun shines bright in this part
A pleasant day encouraging a good start
Various interests has 'Bracklesham Bay'
Giving old and young a pleasant day
They may wish to collect fossils
Which to many folk appeals
Early morn along shores filled with dew
They dream of finding something new
There are also folk not so young
Taking to the sea for their plunge

Winter comes and most folk battle with snow
When life in 'Bracklesham Bay' is all aglow
As soon as spring is on its way
Folk come towing various boats to the bay
Some often getting into a knot
Trying to find themselves a good spot
A sight very happy and gleeful
Until the day becomes cool
Evening brings magnificent sunsets aglow
Then 'stillness' as the sun sinks low.

Josephine Foreman

After The Storm

The sea spumes over the rocks in the foreland
Spurred on by the frantic storm, it roared on its way
O'er the tors on the moorland, just as the day was born.
It panicked the horses, and ruffled the sheep,
And the grouse from their secret rests,
The villagers awoke from their dreamless sleep
While birds flew high from their nests.

In the wake of the wind, and the darkening sky
Came the rain torrential and grey,
And the echoing screech of the curlews cry,
As they circled around the bay.
Almost as sudden as it began, it abated its fury spent
Then out came the sun, wintry and cool
And a rainbow, magic! Heaven sent!

The water now translucent, and white in the ebbing storm,
Creams soft o'er the stones on the rain washed beach
In the calm of the late May morn.
Now a soft summer breeze whispers high in the pines
And a forest of trees nod their heads,
While the flowers now wait for the sun on their faces
As the late spring and warm summer weds!

Marie Bowerman-Taylor

Orphan Babe

Cry not my little one
The hand of comfort clasp
Your plight may seem a sorry one
Yet joy's within your grasp

Little orphan baby
The world seems not to care
But someone will be waiting
For an answer to a prayer

Two kindly loving souls
Who would prefer none other
Than to take you for their own
Be your father and your mother.

Sheila Scott

THE ISABELLE PLANTATION IN MAY

In Richmond's royal park you'll find
A woodland garden quite divine
The scent of flowers fills the air
To greet you as you enter there
Beneath the old gnarled oak tree
Lilies of the valley blooming free
Amid bluebells and anemone
A gentle stream meanders through
Flanked by flowers of every hue
And in the crystal waters flow
Primulas, irises and kingcups grow
A riot of colour the azaleas provide
Along the banks on either side
In the glades around the stream
Flowering rhododendron trees
Add more beauty to the scene
The trickle of water and the song of a bird
The only sounds that can be heard
A haven of peace and solitude
To put you in a tranquil mood.

Edith Blake

A Week In Herefordshire (In Autumn)

Blissfully peaceful and quiet, a place to
Relax and slow down.
In an area that old Mother Nature, has
Wrapped in her wonderful gown.

Quite close to the beautiful Malvern Hills,
Not far from the forest of Dean . . .
The countryside here, at this time of the
Year, believe me, just has to be seen.

We have spent seven glorious days here
But alas we are now homeward bound . . .
Refreshed, and with memories we will never forget,
Of the peace and the friendship we found.

J Gay

A Promise To Flo

One thing there is that I can justly take
Not purposing aught in return to give
As long as on this earth I still can live
And seemingly one-sided bargains make;

There underneath your soft eye whence it came
I find it on your cheek . . . soft also . . . lying
Though dignity subdues your silent crying,
That single tear is waiting just the same.

It waits for me, before it disappears,
To bend and with my lips now make it mine.
This taking without giving is the sign
That through me you will have no cause for tears.

Peter S A Cooper

Our Friend The Beech Tree

The beech tree in our garden
Is fifty feet high or more
And every spring its
Pale green leaves and branches
Sweep gently to the floor.
And in the summer it gives us shade
Where cream teas are taken
With cakes home made.
And in the autumn its leaves are shed
Like a child in its pyjamas
Getting ready for its bed.
And in the winter it sleeps content,
Disregarding the winter's element,
Through snow and wind, hail and rain.
And in the spring awakens
To start all over again.

Dennis R Beton

February Gems

Frosty diamonds, white opals and pearls
Glisten and gleam as daylight unfurls
Nothing can equal that glorious sight
Of February frost that comes overnight.

The dewdrops all gleam with silver and gold
And cobwebs sparkle with crystals untold,
Those stars of the morning how brightly they shine
They are the treasures of God's precious mine.

But these jewels of heaven so soon melt away
He gives but a glimpse at the break of the day.

Winnie Sands

Old Age Should Always Be Enjoyed And Never Suffered

Old age often causes us to suffer many ills,
sadly we may also lose some talents and some skills.
Wouldn't it be great if this were not the case?
Instead of stepping down a gear we quickened up our pace!
If we became more able with every passing year,
we'd look forward to a future with not so much to fear.
People thinking we were old would bring about great pleasure,
and seeing ourselves ageing is something we would treasure.
Climbing up steep mountains would no longer be a chore,
we'd very quickly reach the top and still be fit for more.
When grandchildren came visiting it's true beyond all doubt,
our energy and liveliness would surely wear them out!
And when the time came to retire due to such good health,
we'd be fit enough to benefit from all our hard earned wealth.
To be less able than our offspring would be extremely rare,
so we'd never need to worry about being put in care.
Eventually the day would come when we'd begin to find,
thoughts of starting a new life were always on our mind.
Soon after this prepared for death with loved ones by our side,
contentedly we'd leave this world feeling full of pride.
Relations would remember us with very high regard,
knowing that to match our strength was always very hard.

Y Campbell

Love's Unkind

Something in the moonlight catches my eye,
As I see it's you walking by
My legs turn to jelly,
My heart misses a beat,
Could you be the one I seek?

You smile at me and things get worse,
I really feel like I'm going to burst!
But then I realise that loves unkind,
As I watch your behind.

Angela Macfarlane

THROUGH THE WATERFALL

(To my special friend Andrea)

Looks like I've passed, these desert storms,
Beyond where, darkened shadows dawn.
And through the waterfall of dreams,
To find this land, of pastures green.

No longer do I stand alone,
Upon these bloody battle grounds.
For you are there, with sword in hand,
To help me win, and make a stand.

Blades flash swift, in moonlit night,
Our hearts are strong to help us fight.
A passion free; the dragon falls,
No longer burns these castle walls.

The crow flies high,
As darkness fails.
The good you give, helped me prevail.
You give me strength and company,
And all these things, I give to thee.

Chris Edwards

INSIDE-OUT AT INNERWYKE

Sunshine, floods this brighter room,
Billowing out, dark night times gloom.
As if night time was never here!
How come we paint the dark with fear?
As sometimes, in our beds we lay,
We mark each sound till break of day?
Till break of day, each creak and knock,
Till break of day, minds phantoms, shock!

Now bright windows, frame blue skies,
In a glimpse - a sunlit seabird flies;
Above a new day's traffic sounds,
Below on street-wise postman rounds,
Where walking, driving: bus or bike,
Some kid named Joe? Some guy - like Mike?
Till twilight time, fun, stress and strife.
Till twilight time, they lead this life!

Whilst I, meanwhile in limbo torn,
In convalescence, to the manor borne;
In Innerwyke, slightly out of place,
In Innerwyke, like outer space!
To await on high, in Innerwyke,
Outside, Felpham street lights flick,
On and on, and in my mind.
Blake, and others, lived, worked, slept,
Before; where night's long shadows crept,
Eclipsed to west, sunset divides.
At Innerwyke, till darkness flies,
Till Innerwyke nights, meets dawn's sunrise.

Paul Nicklin

The Girl Of My Dreams

Your eyes so bright,
your body so light,
and so I must redeem,
you're the girl of my dream.

You're so gentle and kind,
so loving in your mind,
my love it seems
because you're the girl of my dream.

Your hair so tidy and neat,
you're like a queen, when you take a seat,
my love for you is full steam,
because you're the girl of my dream.

You're like a baby doll,
you're my life and soul,
I'm deeply in love it seems,
with you the girl of my dream.

Steve Wright

I Was A Traffic Warden Many Years Ago

I was a traffic warden for more years than I can remember
But that was many years ago and life's now a dying ember.
I miss the friends I worked with and never see them now
Like me they have gone their separate ways
And like that old time melody, it's a long long while
From May to September
And I haven't got time for the waiting game.

A Cook

THE WINDSOR BOAT TRIP

To the Thames side at Windsor by coach,
Boarding the open top deck of the launch;
Slatted seats fore and aft, chose the bow
For shade, by the large canopy blue.

The wheel house amidships with captain;
Gold rings in the ears of two crewmen,
One had a coloured 'kerchief tied,
Bare chest, bare feet; buccaneer implied!

This pirate hand cast off the mooring,
Heading upstream, our horn sounding warning:
Launches of various shapes, colour, size;
Peak of the season, all sorts caught our eyes.

We settle down, our day to enjoy,
Many the scenes for eyes to employ;
Swans, geese, ducks; moorhens as well
Foraging, away from the channel.

Broveney Lock: we tie up mid stream,
Awaiting discharge of vessels down stream:
Sparkling white water, from backwater weir;
Near bank lined with craft queuing there.

A delightful scene while in the lock,
The garden ablaze with colourful stock;
In contrast, the grass was luscious green,
Sprinklers playing to keep its sheen.

Leaving Bray, we see approaching the locks,
Rowing boats, each had four oarsmen and cox;
College lads we thought them to be,
Return to Eton from practice spree.

At Maidenhead our river trip ends:
Coach is waiting to take us to friends,
Mr and Mrs Michael, for tea on their lawn;
Renewed love of Christ, sweet and warm.

Cyril Skeet

TEA BREAK

He did you know, did you hear?
All over town from 'ere to 'ere.
She did you know, have you heard?
Well, how silly, how absurd.
Have you seen them both together?
No, you're kidding, No, and I saw letters.
Did you see? No . . . Oh yes I did,
it was his fault, I'm sure he did.
Was it them on such a day?
Yes, thingy said she didn't pay.
It wasn't hers you know, that coat!
Oh go on, you silly goat.
What do yer think about their car?
I only saw it from afar.
Bet it was nicked. I've heard it said
their bank account's way in the red.
Well to be sure, it's just come clear
he's always drunk and it aint on beer.
Smokes like a trooper. Where'd he get the money?
Same place as 'er though I think it's rummy.
Well I must go my tea break's up . . .
Oh won't you stay for another cup.
No, but I so enjoy our gossip,
pin your ears for a few more topics.
Byeeeeee . . .

Faith Perry

Kerry

I miss her cold wet nose upon my face,
As she licked me clean at her own pace.
Her big brown eyes so sad and round,
Used to open wide when I made a sound.
Her tail would wag from side to side,
Cleaning my carpet with one slide.
I never moaned that wouldn't be right,
As she kept me happy day and night.
By bringing me gifts that she had found,
Her favourite was a bone she had dug out the ground.
A dirty shoe a smelly sock,
It didn't matter she brought the lot.
I think she thought I was her pup,
Me and her used to cuddle up.
But now she's gone to doggie heaven,
I still miss her now I'm eleven.
In my dreams I see her run,
And in that dream we have lots of fun.

Kayleigh Rhodes (11)

Dawn

Awaken sun and arise in the midnight sky,
Shower the world in golden rays.
Alight all the trees,
Remove all the shade.
Awaken birds from peaceful rest,
call up a dawn chorus,
To awaken the rest.
Let the stars and moon fade away,
As night gives way to day.

Angela Grace

A Pebble Beach

Jewelled coloured stones are washed by the shifting brine,
relentlessly, never ceasing, throughout time.
Nylon snakes left by thoughtless man,
lie with driftwood and a rusting can.
Small boats wait shackled to the shore,
until they sail the blue green depths once more.
They disappear but return with the changing tide,
a human figure cocooned safe inside.
The wind gusts carrying salt spray in the air,
through the Shrubby Seablite clinging to life there.
This is a harsh place, it's wild and free,
this pebble beach beside the sea.

Karen Hutton

Thee My Love

Thee my love hath long gone
To a far better place in the far beyond
Will show them what an angel you are
Just glint and glow like the brightest star
Will be able to spot you on starry nights
Hanging there shining your angel light
Time has taken its toll of us all
That's when the raindrops start to fall.

Thee my love hath long gone
With all those beautiful angels where you belong
Do you remember the time we first met?
Our love together I'll never regret
You even shined like an angel in those days
Like a Madonna arisen in full display
An angel long gone from me
Some day darling I'll come and stay with thee.

Raymond J Bullock

Agony Of A Fox

Shivering in his parental den,
Hearing the sharp barks of the dogs
On their way to a morning's sport on the fen,
His mother out to find him food in the bogs,
Make light his heart, poor lonely fox.

Scurrying around the ground by his den,
Wondering whether he will see his mother
Again, hearing the clop clop of the horses hooves, when
He dared to listen, he hears a whine
His mother's call to hide poor lonely fox.

Tramping of heavy hooves and padding of dogs by his den,
Heart filled with terror will he see his mother again;
Thoughts of starving fills his troubled heart when,
Cries of a fox is heard loudly behind the den,
His heart misses a beat poor lonely fox.

Hearing the tearing of the screaming fox,
Hiding his head under his paws in his den,
Mother! Mother! May it not be you inside the box
Of yelping hounds fighting each other on the fen,
Hoping to hear his mother's call poor lonely fox.

A shout of '*heel*' came to his sharp ears,
'Away with you, you bloody dogs',
Yelping and howling came to his terror filled silent gears?
Tucked tightly together in trembling clogs,
Once more he was alone poor lonely fox.

Out of the den he stealthily trod,
Keeping well in the shadows after the hunt had gone.
No sign of his mother could he espy on the bog,
A shake of his head and a whine that she alone,
Would know, sadly, he wandered off
to find perhaps a friend; poor lonely fox.

Alma Montgomery Frank

MEMORIES

As I sit here alone on a Sunday noon,.
My heart is heavy so full of gloom,
I've a roast in the oven heaven knows why,
When all I want is to curl up and die.

Lunch time on Sunday was great in the past,
We'd go to the local for a jolly good laugh!
A glass or two of our favourite brew -
Walk home arm in arm, that's what we'd do.

Fill our tummies with good home cooked grub,
Leave the dishes for later, go to bed and make love,
Get up and wash all the greasy pans,
A nice cup of tea to refresh our glands.

Have a lovely hot bath, don our Sunday best,
Then where did we go? I bet you have guessed!
We couldn't dine out, or go to a show,
Run a car, have a holiday, as wages were low.

Sadly we get older, then one passes on -
You just cannot grasp how the past years have gone.
Stunned with shock, nearly out of your mind,
Why not a ticket for two, at the end of the line.

I suppose one adjusts to a life on their own,
At the moment it's hard, feel I can't go it alone,
We can't plan our destiny, perhaps a good thing,
You never can tell what tomorrow will bring.

Rose Gilder

Cottage Industry

In a cottage through a glade sits an old man encased in blankets
to keep him warm, reflects his life and once what was.
His dog it looks as old as he, sits by his chair only movement made
is a stir
from his master and he would respond with upward glance in
saddened stare.
Through window panes soiled by weather, shines the sun casting
shadows which
move faster than the occupants of the room.
Beams of light protrude on curled up photographs wilting on the
mantelpiece
above an unlit fire, hold their secrets of who they were and in part
of life they once played.
Paintings tilt on walls they hang, cobwebs grace gilded frames, spots
of acid
Marks on inner mounts that dress the now fading artists disappearing
work.
Once proud to achieve and brought along to the cottage in the glade
by himself
to receive his pay. Here the industry was bread, baked and sold to
the village near.
Three o'clock each day the ovens lit and doe in them at four
would go.
Family up and all at work each his duty to perform, the horse now
fed attached
to cart his payload baskets full of bread, off through bumpy lanes
would head.
The bustling market place would reach for another busy day to end
in sale
and return with empty cart to house in glade.

The years would pass in need no more of cottage industry, as them, and each
would watch each other pass and doe the ovens not receive but rust the oven
doors ceased and memories fell to join the dust upon the floors.
Now stirred the old man in his chair, remembering these the happy years
that now have passed, opens eye to down his cheek release one last tear.

Christopher Poynter

YOU FILL MY HEART

Oh heavenly Father if I could say what I feel in my heart
I don't know where to start.
The words seem so far away
'Oh Father' you fill my heart
When I see the sunshine, the flowers
The gentle breeze blowing thro' the trees
What would the world be like without such beauty
Can such beauty control our destiny?
Only the touch of Your hands
In this world so full of sorrow through man's own failing
Only the touch of the Master's hands
Will help them see the error of their ways,
Look forward to happier days
There are millions of people need you 'Oh Lord'
In this world full of cruelty and greed.
As the days come and go, you fill my heart.
We must all play our part.
Always find time to pray at the end of the day.

Eva Rusher

The Golden Oldies

There's a couple in our street,
that I'd like you all to meet,
or rather should I just say 'get to know',
they are short and rather weighty,
and they're both well over eighty,
they can tell you many tales of long ago.

Now the tale that can be told is,
they have joined the 'golden oldies',
which is a club for folk just in their prime,
in fair or stormy weather you will find them there together,
and they'll tell you that they have a lovely time.

I should like you all to know,
that not so very long ago,
they realised that life can't be all fun,
there's a wealth of love out there,
in which these oldies share,
for the love of God is there for everyone.

He is always there to guide us,
and we need Him here beside us,
He knows what's in our hearts at any time,
I thank the Lord above for His everlasting love,
and remember, He's our Father, yours and mine.

So if it's fellowship you're after,
combined with love and laughter,
and you wonder if you'll find it - yes, you will,
if you'd really like to know,
where these 'golden oldies' go,
just ring the church and simply ask for Phyll.

Edith Robinson

After The Play

It's our first night together.
We've just been to a play
About unhappy families.
In bed you shyly say:
'I talk to mother's photograph
When I wake up each day.

She passed away two years ago'.
How do I reply?
That I, too, talk to photographs?
No. That would be a lie.

My truth: I feared my mother.
That feeling drove out love.
I watched her die, but couldn't cry.
No help came from 'above'.

Sudden tears are in your eyes.
Dulling their soft blue.
I sense our childhood paths ran close.
(Enchanted days were few).

'I think' you said 'Ma loved me.'
I never was quite sure.
I know I disappointed her.
She once said 'You're impure!'
She knew from early on, you see
I might well be gay.
Though, darling, I need women too,
So *please* don't walk away.

As if I could. I love you like
A longed-for elder brother.
I'll be both girl *and* boy for you,
And play, sometimes, *the mother*.

Elizabeth Mark

November Sea

No sand castles are left upon the shore;
No longer do the children shout with glee.
Their spades and buckets can be seen no more.

Two surfers brave the powerful pounding sea,
their wet suits shining in a watery glow.
With sudden swoops and graceful movements free

they sail upon the waves. The ebb and flow
of water seems to share their winter fun,
and sand and pebbles swirl about below

their surfboards. When their exercise is done
they stagger clumsily upon the land,
across the seaweed and the rocky stones.

A fisherman is digging in the sand
looking for bait to drop into his pail,
pausing every now and then to stand.

And stretch and listen to the seagull's wail.
No sunset lights the sky and all is grey;
all nature seems to tell a winter's tale.

As evening falls, I must no longer stay;
I choose a pebble, marked with pretty ring
and pass the little beach huts on my way.

A chilly mist is shrouding everything:
Does early winter mean an early spring?

Joanna Young

'EVERGREEN' AEROBICS

Every day the leisure centre changing rooms
Are filled with specimens of sporting prowess
That is, except Wednesday mornings,
When they ring with cries of 'Hello, Bess!'

It's the Evergreen's aerobics class
Where they're old, unfit and resigned to fate
Most are there by doctors' orders
Though many suspect it's a little too late.

But every Wednesday morning, there they are
Zimmer frames abandoned, ready to go
Twenty old ladies (and Mr Crotchly)
Wrinkles and pimples put out on show.

Bemused by the loud pop music
They go up, down, one, two, three
Obeying the orders of their instructor
A lycra-clad 'babe' (twenty three).

'Fit! I feel fit for nothing!' they grumble
And 'Slow down! My heart's giving me gyp!'
One by one they crumble
With cries of 'Oh! My bad hip!'

The instructor glares on, unsympathetic,
As the oldies puff, pant and sigh
Gwyneth's lost her hearing aid
The rest feel ready to die.

At last the ordeal is over
They feel coming was a mistake
Now it's off to the cafeteria
For a slice of double chocolate cake!

Hannah Marder (13)

Thank You For Being Grandma

You were a grandma, mum and daughter
Aunt, cousin, niece and wife
Spreading love and happiness
Each role fitted in your life

Your greatest role was grandma
Or are we being unfair
As that is how we knew you
Our grandma of love and care

You and grandad were the perfect couple
Loving each other dearly
You doted on us three grandchildren
Loving us all sincerely

We have so many beautiful memories
Of spending time with you
Of playing all our favourite games
Cards and bingo to name but a few

Of running around your nurtured garden
Of playing for hours in the park
Of cuddling up and watching telly
When it came to dark

Of fish and chips in the cafe
Of days spent on the beach
Special memories will never fade
All are in perfect reach

One last thing to thank you for
Is for having a special child
Our mother, your daughter, the light of your life
Is to put it mild

We know she is missing you daily
Right to the end you gave her fun
She gives us so much happiness
Thank you for choosing our mum

We hope that people will remember you
In lots of different ways
But to us it was as our special grandma
We will love you always.

Nikki Burton

POETRY OF POETS

One two three plus thousands more you see
One of which I am I think? Yes sir that's me
Born in the county of Middlesex has to be
There once was a small village name of which yes
Was Isleworth to myself one of the very best
Born in the year of 1917 a war baby you could say
The name of the street I did live if I may
Tell you all was number forty eight South Street was then
Until they had them demolished that was the day
South Street was a very narrow street to be sure
A said street of shopkeepers door to door.

Just off this street was name of Worple Road see
Of that road say no more - except a police station to be
A local bobby maybe a couple more? To stop one from
Breaking the law - not much chance of that in those days
Of old - well you did not hear of any in stories told
A lovely village with plenty of history of royalty
Arriving at Syon House the Duke of Northumberland to visit
Yes sir (he) - that said house was and still is in
Syon Park - visited by queens and a certain king
None other than King Henry VIII just had to be
I have put you in the picture so to speak of our county
The county of my birth my name is just Tom (Sexton) that's me.

T Sexton

Moment In Time

We drank shandy, and ate sausages, in the car park at 'The Bull';
We had music on the radio, - Elvis, Cliff, and Sandie Shaw;
You phoned your mum to ask about your daughter, and found that
all was well;
Then we returned to the shaded car, relaxed and kissed across the
steering wheel
and drank again whilst chuckling on the foibles of our petty jobs
where often we had met in formal circumstance:
. . .And finally we made love; strange, contorted, furtive, illicit,
caressing, delectable love:
Never before had the thrill of that ultimate consummation been so
sweet
for two such searching souls, both coming from the emotional
wastelands
of their respective homes.
And after that we straightened our clothes,
took the glasses back, then bade the place farewell.
We stopped at Rotherhithe for our final snog,
bought 'sav an' chips twice', saw that huge rat;
and home you hurriedly went to beat the midnight chimes.

On Monday morning, Miss A was back at her first floor typing desk
and Mr B in his stuffy third floor office.
Lies had been told,
pretences had been erected, and nobody had been hurt
. . . except ourselves; because we knew it couldn't go on.
But I'll never forget that beautiful evening at 'The Bull'.
I hope *you* won't, Miss A, . . . *wherever* you are.

E J Parke

UNTITLED

Life is great of that I know
Yet the sorrow in my face shows
I lost so much my children too
Life is hard yet happy too.

Listen to the birds they sing
there's so much happiness they bring
to look up in the sky and see
how wonderful it must be
to be so free.

J Hartley

DREAMS

My wildest dream to become famous one day
First step, writing poetry to send me on my way
Or maybe an amateur dramatic group
Another strong growing root.
Perhaps my love for singing in my local
I don't really have that bad vocals!

Wish I could play some musical instrument, what a shame!
But then I don't need to play for fame
I could easily have learned one at school
Imagine playing in the Royal Albert Hall!

To appear in a West End musical show
Would also be nice
So many dreams to make my choice, I'll throw a dice
I'm sure many others would wish a dream come true
If we all gave each other a push, I'm sure we'll
Get coming what's due.

Lesley Cebula

FINDING FACE

There was a man who had no face
Now, wasn't that a great shame, indeed, a disgrace?
This man who lived in great splendour and style -
Walked indoors on floors of blue marbled tiles.
He looked out through stained glassed windows at the rest of us
His gardeners and maids beautified his empire; they made such a fuss!
We would, in awe, stare at him from a great distance
Our children, curious but timid and shy, looked at his palace as they passed by - askance.
He was such an imposing figure in our quiet neighbourhood
The local people always thought that he was up to no good
This rather lofty man who had no face
Sat in his aviary, quite often, admiring the beautiful birds beside his
plump wife dressed in yards of antique lace.

This rather lofty man who had no face
Began to show an interest in our neighbourhood ,'The Friendly Place'
He planted oak, palm, cedar and many other types of tree
And introduced a new product which rid our cats and dogs of all their fleas.
He provided food and shelter for the hungry and homeless
Fined the lackadaisical drivers who were so careless
He ensured that the buses and trains all ran on time
And brought to our village tea parties, many varieties of cheese, red and white wines.
We were so amazed at and fascinated by this new man, still with no face
Who had made such a remarkable difference to our new 'Beautiful, Friendly Place'
That we thought that he should be able to smell, hear, taste, touch and see
To be a part of our community - to be just like you and me.

Our artists give him eyes of blue, hair of gold and a noble chin
And at last he could recognise us and were able to notice him
So happy is he to be one of us after having had no face
And we are so delighted that we were instrumental in his admission to the human race.

Margaret Andrews

Gran's Shopping Day

She comes out of the house
Locks the door and shuts the gate
She must hurry the bus will not wait
She is going shopping
The bags are on her arm
Some people passing by give her a smile
With a twinkle in their eye
She is a bit bent
With a hole in her stocking
And people are passing by, and not stopping
She worries about the hair that's not there
She has done her shopping and has had a chat
To one lady and another about this and that
It has made her day
That laugh and chat
Home again she turns the key
And opens the door
She is back and it's time to unpack
She has had a laugh with friends and a chat
Now it's time to relax
She thinks of the ones that are
No longer there and she falls asleep
In her own armchair and thinking
Of all the love she gets elsewhere.

Grace R H Bean

The Magical Bicycle

There was a young boy called Mike,
Who found a magical bike,
He looked at it up,
And he looked at it down,
Then he found himself in a Victorian town.
He jumped on the bike and the bike went fast,
And then he realised he was in the past.
So he carried on riding down the lane,
This old bike was rather a pain,
He rode off to World War II
Where he saw some fighting
But when he tried to move again
He was struck by lightning.
He rode on to see Hitler put a gun to his head,
Just then he wished he was tucked up in bed.
He pedalled to see people having fun,
Then he stopped and bought an iced bun.
He pedalled along with his bun in one hand,
And said 'I want to get out of this land'.
He went past Stone-Age and Vikings too -
He cycled up Pyramids and to Timbuktu
He travelled home and told his mum
He told his dad and everyone,
No-one believed him or his journey,
Only his little brother Ernie!

Lorna Sharman (12)

Cat Burglar

The sound of a door closing,
The scratch on the window pane,
It must just be the wind blowing -
Or has it started to rain?

There's that eerie sound again.
It seems to be very close.
It must be the wind and the rain
Or perhaps a passing ghost!

The sound of a creaking floorboard,
A pounding noise in my head?
A tug on my dressing gown cord!
It's just the cat coming to bed!

Helen Cronin

FISHING

There was a man in a boat,
It was cold so he wore a coat.
'There's something wrong I'm thinking'
Said the sun, whilst he was winking.
The man threw a line to fish,
A big one, Oh! how he wished.
He sat for hours, a bit of a lark,
All of a sudden, he hooked a shark!
A tug and a pull, Oops! that's not fair,
He found himself in the air.

The fish was caught and racing,
The man was following, chasing.
'There *is* something wrong' said the sun,
The man had become undone!
'I'll hold on tight for a bit'
Said the man, he wished he could sit.
Pulled by the fish for a mile or two,
He's fed up now, what should he do?
The man dropped his rod, he had a rest.
Then went back to the boat called the-
Mary Celeste . . . ?

G Dymock

Lovely To Be Loved

It was lovely to be loved by you dear
'Too young, too young' was all we could hear
I was only fifteen a trusting age. 'Blind' they said
Was eighteen when we were wed
We had two daughters and later a son
They brought us happiness and lots of fun
We worked together on the farm land
Life wasn't always what we planned
We had our ups and downs, as the years passed by
But it doesn't help to sit down and cry
Just pull together you'll make it in the end
Simply knowing on each other you can depend
Our children grew up, got married, made their own way in life
We were alone again, just man and wife
Your health gave out you had to retire
For five long years you sat by the fire
We'd been married forty six years when you passed away
I'll never forget that awful day
I've been a widow for eighteen years now
Life just had to go on somehow.
I have lovely memories to treasure
Grandchildren and great grandchildren bringing pleasure
Memories of our wonderful love, dear
Showing them we were not too young, so there.

A Childs

Two Gods

I'm the system that you cannot beat,
I'm forbidden fruit you want to eat.
I'm the virus upon your screen,
I'm the pain before you bleed.

I'm the original media lie,
I'm the day that freedom died.
I'm the love that never lasts,
I'm the test of faith you never passed.

I'm the ozone that's now deplete,
I'm the taste of revenge that is so sweet.
I'm the fear lurking in your heart,
I'm waiting for you in the dark.

G Parker

Looking Ahead To The Wonderful Cleansed Earth

What sheer beauty to behold,
The towering mountains, Oh so bold!
Nooks and crags and snow white peaks,
And many wandering, grazing sheep.

Far in the valley down below,
Sparking, rushing, all aglow,
Waters weaving, cool and clear,
Over large stepping stones and weir.

On either side tall waving trees,
Across the meadow, humming bees.
The sun sheds rays of warmth and light,
A group of birds hover, then take flight.

The scene is one of serenity and peace,
For God has caused all wars to cease.
No more will man pollute the land,
The earth is cleansed by God's own hand.

E Cooke

PEOPLE AS MAKERS OF THE WORLD

Wherever I am, wherever I go - I have so many people around me
. . . so,
There is a question!
Why is it that people differ so much?
And what is it that makes them either cruel and horrible or polite
and kind,
Yes! That question has been for years occupying my mind,
Is it their background, their characters or other factors,
Such as good or bad manners or generally speaking their approach to
life,
I think that people should change their attitude and become more
understanding of each other,
Instead of losing their scruples, especially whilst climbing their
career ladders,
Once they're high positioned or having some power,
They become ruthless - almost a humanless tower
Of strength - with love just for money . . .
Yes! We live in the world of materialism, with no room for
kindness, gentleness or any sentimentalism,
Of course! There are some people who try to shout against all of it
. . . but they act in vain,
For greed, envy, hatred, and lawlessness move in the fast lane,
It's sad but true - unfortunately it is a general point of view,
People were, are, and will be the victims of circumstances,
It could be a political system, a law - which gives them or does not
give them chances
To speak up for their rights, often simply for their survival,
Maybe it should all be changed . . .
But how? - Completely new ideas, perhaps, the whole world
rearranged?
But we have to live *now* and to the best we can - that's the whole
meaning,
And have to start to treat each other with respect, *equally* - just like
one being,
And life would be more bearable, the world would not be so
hostile,

So . . .is it really possible? Would it all reconcile?
I *still* believe in people, the depths of mind and soul,
For without having this belief it will be worthless to stay alive at all.

A Bayless

Out In The Country (Stanton Harcourt Lane)

'Tween field and valley, moor and glen,
Far away from mortal man,
Where shoot and bud in spring began
And horizons shimmer in the sun;
'Neath the darkened copper beech
Where tendrils stretch the sky to reach,
And heaving seas of golden wheat
Dip and sway beside my feet
Is where I'd like to stay a while
To find a face with friendly smile,
Having walked the weary miles
And climbed a host of agèd stiles.
To hear the pheasant's throaty rasp
And see him strutting wingèd past,
To wend the forest's winding path
And wait for shadows, come at last.
E'en when snow and rain doth fall
And winter's winds do howl and call
For frost to creep and crack the wall
And freeze the water in the pail;
Here lies the balm to soothe the spirit,
The heart and mind, and all that's in it.
So pour it out and do not spill it
And fill it to the brim.

Nicky Cooper

Woe! Woe! Never Fear, Mother Is With You

Woe! Woe! Never fear, *Mother* is with you
To save all your screaming souls and caress you
The pigs and the cows
That never knew how
They fell victims to such pains
With knives that sliced through their veins
And do not forget the chicken and sheep
Condemned to deep darkness and left to weep
Oh! If only I could hold and caress all beasts
Just to sit and shed my tears at all your feet
Hauled up by chains, your blood splashes forth and *'men'* eat you
Woe! Woe! Never fear, *Mother* is with you.

Rajeev Bhargava

My Land

Beautiful county, I'm glad you're mine.
Unspoilt in many ways by changing time.
County of hills, villages with ponds, and thatch.
Kindly people, open and friendly, you'd go far to match.
In woodlands you stroll, or to the top of a hill,
Nothing to stop you gazing, or musing at will.
Gardens tended with care, lanes wander, quiet and narrow.
Hours can be spent, listening to nature, nothing to harrow.
Ancient and stately homes, farmland and good old pubs.
Much to find away from life's hurley burley!
Sure to calm you, avoid dying early!
Here in the Chilterns, from my cradle to my grave
I'll stay; Oh! by the way,
Read the first letter of every line,
Enigma resolved! you'll know this county of mine.

Jane Uff

MIDDLESEX

Middlesex is the county in which I have lived all my life,
During which time I have been through much strife
In the county, King Hussein, Byron and Leo Amery went to
Harrow School
And the last pushed Leo Amery into the swimming pool.
There is a stadium at Wembley
Which from my upstairs classroom I could see
It was the first home of Queen Mary's dolls house,
In which an elephant would be in scale the size of a mouse.
George V made the first broadcast
But by no means the last
Of a reigning king
At the British Empire exhibition of which many praises
people did sing
Every year people at Wembley play football,
The attraction of which I cannot see at all.
Wembley also contains Barn Hill,
Which made me feel really ill
When on cross-country, I had to run up it
And I was left feeling a lack of wit
When I got lost twice
And felt worse than lice.
My own town Kenton was the original home
Not, I hasten to add, of the Wembley Dome
But of radio's Dr and Mrs Dale
Who eventually put their home up for sale
And moved to Parkwood Hills
From where to patients, he continued to dispense pills.
Middlesex is where I have always lived.

Sunil Hiranandani

From Ronsard

When you are old and calm, too calm for tears
You'll take my book, and reading by the fire
Be young again. My love, my bright desire
Shall lift awhile the barrier of the years.
But who will see, or heed your beauty still
When I am gone, and all my lovely praise
Has spent itself and died? Oh! then who will
Remain to hear you speak of splendid days?
I shall be dead, my now most urgent frame
Silent amidst the myrtle and the earth.
And you regretting more your high disdain
Will crave the love I offered. But the fame
Of life's proud joy holds but the moment's worth.
The summer's rose cannot be winter's gain.

L J Montgomery

Springtime Is For Lovers

When you fall in love at springtime
It will last though years go by
For springtime is for lovers
And love that will never die

When the first flower blooms in spring
So love will blossom to
For springtime is for lovers
Just like me and you

Birds sings merrily in springtime
They sing sweet songs of love
For springtime is for lovers
And a real and lasting love

Sheila Chimes

Is One Day Enough?

There is one day in the year,
That you express your feelings for the one that is so dear.
You buy gifts and cards to show your love,
But is one day really enough?

What happens on all those other days?
Do you show them how you feel in other ways?
Or do they get taken for granted,
And you just pretend, the words 'I love you' have been said?

Do you just assume they know how you feel?
Or do you make sure they know your love is real?
Do you try to make everyday as special as you can?
And if not, you should try and make it your plan.

Make sure you tell the person you love what they mean to you,
Don't leave them in any doubt give them a clue.
Show your feelings all year round and not just on that one day,
Don't hold yourself back, let the words of love have their say.

Don't leave them second guessing,
Make sure it is clear what you are expressing.
Put your feelings into words,
Loud enough to be heard.

Don't let your words be misunderstood,
Tell the one you love all you know you should.
Don't leave it until that one day a year,
To make your true feelings clear.

K Hall

LOST ENGLAND

Lost men, of far forgotten pride, ne'er
'Walk upon England's mountains green'
Fallen ruins of a nation bleeding,
Divided by sunken words, each utters deserted
To fortress barren walls.

Come last the wicket, fallen silent
'On England's pleasant pastures seen'
Honour gouged in blooded, senseless flags;
Heads bowed low, to mark respect
Of England's dirtied, kneeling, resign!

Did we not hear
'Among these dark satanic mills'
England's farewell sigh
Said o'er dying lands
Countrymen tread in fear.

Where now,
'In England's green and pleasant land'
Lay we nights in quiet sleep,
Of safety granted, by swords raised high
In so restless, abusing isle!

R Ives

JUST A SHELL

You're looking at me, but only the shell
You have no idea of the tales I can tell
As I sit here and look up at the sky
I remember the first time I saw a plane fly

The transport went from horses to cars
And now they are sending up rockets to Mars
The phone and TV are remarkable things
With records I can still hear Caruso sing

I used to love it when we all wore long dresses
And ladies had maids to tend to their tresses
Now it's hard to tell the boys from the girls
It seems that the boys have the long hair and curls

I sometimes sit here and I shed a few tears
But then I remember the wonderful years
I wish I could talk, there is so much to tell
But since I had my stroke, there is only a shell

Carol A Maddison

DAUGHTERS' TEETH

Into the bathroom like good girls,
Duty bound to brush those pearls.
The three of them all different ages,
Their pure white teeth at special stages.

For Amy, eight have been and gone,
They're now grown up teeth, clean and strong.
To Amy's room the fairy's been, never heard and never seen.
When through her window day comes creeping,
Upon a coin Amy's head lies sleeping.

Charlotte brushed the other day and all at once in shock did say,
'This tooth in front, not long' she said, 'Will remain inside my head'
I know the fairies always pay, to take a dear sweet tooth away.
But this one she will not receive I cannot bear to see it leave.

Wobbly teeth and fairies' treasure, Jessie sees and takes great pleasure.
She feels she's missing out somewhere and knows that that is just not fair.
'Look mum, two teeth are out,
Two more wobble, there is no doubt.'
Sadly Jessie's only two, we fear her statement can't be true.

M Dean

What Is Love?

Love can be warm,
Love can be cold,
Love can be young,
Love can be old,
The longer the love
The more mature it is
When you have been together
For years and years,
There must be a secret
How some lovers last,
It could be what's been experienced
In their past,
They seem to know
What to say and do,
To make their love last for years
Through and through.

H Bolton

Spring

Little rays of sun light wakening up the earth
All nature is returning like a second birth,
Little birds' interest turn to building nests
Doing little dances and try to look their best,
Squirrels come out of hiding, stand and look around
And listen to the music of the birds' sweet sound,
The sweet smell of blossom that lingers in the breeze
That makes a gently swaying of the leaves in the trees,
Rabbits are appearing and jumping everywhere
Making all nature realise spring is in the air,
Baby lambs are running across a carpet of green
Everywhere new life is appearing on the scene.

M Ajaib

Dream Land

(For Emily, Jack and Mollie)

Close your eyes and catch a ride,
To dream land, it's up there in the sky.
Where the river flows of fizzy lemonade,
And ice cream flowers grow tall in chocolate rain.

Look at the sun, shining down on Plastercine people
Lick it and taste it, it's made of toffee and treacle.

Count to three, make a wish,
See the jelly green flying fish.
They'll take you home to your sleepy eyes,
Until tomorrow's dream,
And the yellow lemon lollipop surprise.

C Leith

Miss Pym

I would have passed her by without a word.
She spoke, I looked again . . . and memory stirred
Of lecturer retired . . Oh! Years before.
She used to walk her dog along the shore
With springy step . . She dressed with care and style,
She had a lively air, an eager smile . . .
And how she sparkled when she told the ways
She planned to spend those long-earned leisure days!

I sat beside her and we talked awhile.
Her sparkle dulled now and her eager smile
Dissolved in listlessness, she told me how
She'd fallen ill, was in a home and now,
Her savings dwindling, she'd nightly pray
She wouldn't wake to see another day.

Ancient Briton

TRUE BRITS

Can we have some fireworks dad? Can we have a guy?
Can we have some rockets to light up the sky?
Can we have potatoes and chestnuts we can cook?
Can we let the kids next door come and have a look?
They don't have a daddy, so we said that they could share
Makes us feel better when we know that you are there.
They can't buy any fireworks, I said to ask their mum.
She hadn't any money, but can they still come?

Me and Sally said that if the eatables get short
The visitors can have them, we'll do as we ought
Jamie's only three, so he'll have to have his lot
So get the bonfire going, we want it nice and hot
The sky looks very cloudy, it'll very soon be dark
We'll lock the dog safe in the shed, so all he'll do is bark
And if it *does* start raining, we'll take it on the chin
'Cause Jamie says, like picnics, we can have the fireworks *in*!

Doris Holland

A DORSET DAY

I'm starting to soak up the peace and rest in the solitary
air,
There are gliding birds, the tide is moving so slowly it
relaxes my thoughts.
Suddenly the sky goes very grey, but my mind is shining on a
Dorset day.
This place I could describe as heaven,
maybe it is, I don't know, but I will say it is bliss.
I hear birds singing and a shuffle of feet walking behind me,
but I don't turn around, I have nothing to fear, on this Dorset
day everything is wonderfully calm, even graceful on a typical
Dorset day.

Michael Mead

TWIESELDOWN

Just outside Fleet, is Twieseldown -
For me, heaven on earth!
A large piece of army land,
Stretching for miles. Uneven land,
Mostly covered by heather and gorse.
There are also pines; so sweetly scented; pines
Doing their best to prevent strong light
Reaching the ground
They stand on. It springs, it's stony;
One can find fossils, if one takes the time
To look down, to search;
To handle, to scrutinise the stones.
I found a whole sea urchin once!
Twieseldown . . . it's so peaceful there;
It's so peaceful.
Only nature, at its best. Only the birds,
The occasional rabbit . . .
Only the gentle, soothing song of birds.
Only heather; heather and gorse.
Only trees; beeches, silver birches,
Oaks. On Twieseldown there is a small oak,
Standing alone at a certain place -
I always go and see it. I always go.
Nature at its best. Wild rhododendrons, bramble . . .
Seasons pass; berries grow. I pick them; eat them!
I see buds on the heather; then later, flowers.
I rarely meet anyone, on Twieseldown;
Only butterflies cross my path.
Butterflies, ladybirds . . .
Small, delightful things.

Claire-Lyse Sylvester

A Sense Of Humour

(Dedicated to Mike Grogan)

Old Man Time, he waits for no one.
Though it's rather sad to say,
He changes our face to lines of laughter
And our hair a silvery grey.

We face many situations,
Life seems to be a test
Through the hurt and sorrow
Days of joy and happiness.

There is that certain something,
If it remains unchanged
Can help us through the bad times,
Make us smile again.

It can brighten up our attitude,
Make our heart feel light,
Help us face the day again,
Make the world seem bright.

You have that certain magic,
A special gift it's true,
Don't ever lose its quality,
That's such a part of you.

B Sharp

Guardian

I have a spotted cheetah, close beside my bed,
I kid myself he's guarding me, I hope that he's been fed.
He has a fearsome snarling mouth, wide open with sharp teeth,
He sits there staring at me, with carpet underneath.

As I drift off to sleep at night, I dream he moves about,
He goes beyond my garden, to a jungle I've no-doubt.
To swiftly run, his prey to catch, long legs will take him miles,
Apply his wits, outsmart the game, and use his cunning wiles.

Next morning when I am awake, I look across to see,
My guardian - who the night before, was looking after me.
I smile and pat him on the head, 'Well done my trusty friend,'
An ornament he may be, but one I'll never lend.

Beulah Thompson

AUTUMN LEAVES

Glorious the leaves of autumn,
Ruby, russet and rust they fall,
Tawny, topaz and titian red,
Incandescent smouldering gold,
Ochre, copper and chestnut brown,
Terracotta and apricot.
All earthly wisdom in one leaf,
All that withers will be reborn,
Burnished, burning, blazing, flaming,
Falling autumn leaves.

Glorious the leaves of autumn,
Amber, auburn and red they fall,
Soft saffron and burnt sienna,
Incandescent smouldering gold,
Orange, bronze and mahogany,
Mellow honey and marigold,
All earthly wisdom in one leaf,
All that withers will be reborn,
Burnished, burning, blazing, flaming,
Falling autumn leaves.

Denise Margaret Hargrave

Being Ill

When I was ill and lying in bed
And all I could move, was my neck and my head
I look out of the window and what do I see
The birds, the clouds and the top of a tree.

A blackbird rests in the tree's top branches
And sings its song, which enhances
My mind with the sweetness of its song
I look again, the bird has gone.

I hope the blackbird comes again
To sing its song so ease the pain
The pain increases as the day goes on
Oh good! Here is the blackbird to sing its song.

Raindrops on the window pane
The sun tries to shine again
Drops of water run down to the sill
Oh no! Its time for another pill.

And so another day has come and gone
Our feathered friend has sung its song
The wind stops blowing, the rain does cease
Oh! Quiet world, Oh! Eternal peace.

Ron J Wells

Day's End

The sun is now setting, it is low in the sky,
And warmth from its rays is beginning to die,
Clouds upon high, coloured by remnants of glow,
What a wonderful sight, this late evening show.

Reflections in the river shimmer and dance,
A cool evening breeze makes all the trees prance,
And the cry of birds flying home to their nests,
While other creatures, are getting up from their rest.

I can just see the moon so distant and pale,
Starting its journey through the heavenly trail,
It glides under the stars, with their twinkling light,
Shimmering up there for us, all through this night.

Alan Winston Curtis

THE ROCKING HORSE

I started life as a tall oak tree
Until the woodman's axe struck me,
Suddenly I was a big block of wood
And in a timber yard I stood.

Oak and cedar, teak and pine
A motley crowd of us in line
Then I was bought by a new vendor
Whose art and craft restored my splendour.

Many hours he toiled on me
His carving really held the key
Glowing mane and burnished tail
My harness studded with fine detail.

'Tis true I'll never win a race
But in a nursery I've pride of place,
Content and happy now - of course
Because I'm a glorious - *Rocking Horse*

Mavis Johnson

The Fat Belly

I once had a friend who had a fat belly
That would mould to the shape of his seat;
It grew as he munched in front of the telly
And obscured the view of his feet.

This amazing voluminous expandable belly
Could oft' make my friend feel quite queer;
It'd wobble and look like a raspberry jelly
When filled with a gallon of beer!

To appease the demands of this leguminous belly
My friend would exert into a hurry;
With a deft little foot inside each black welly
In pursuit of a suitably hot curry!

To the doctor for advice he once took his large belly
The quack with dismay checked his heart;
To get over the shock he stopped off by the deli
And bought a huge strawberry tart.

'I am to die' he said to his loveable belly
'Unless I stop eating so much grub!'
'Then I'll be thin like ascetic Aunt Nelly
And instead of laughing I'll blub!'

So down went the tart and thank you said belly
In the way that only bellies know how;
With the beer and the curry it was pleasantly smelly
And resembled the sound of a cow!

I'll always remember my friend and his belly -
In life they were merry and mirth;
Sent off to heaven by good Father Kelly
Now marked by a large mound of earth!

Edward Chalmers

My Favourite Things

What are my favourite things?
The sun so bright, the stars
That come out at night
The wind that helps you fly a kite
The countryside where it's
Nice to walk and talk.

What are my favourite things?
The joy a new-born baby brings
The smell of new mown grass
The flowers and the trees
Eating Cheddar cheese.

What are my favourite things
The smile on a child's face
My cat nothing could take her place
Forgetting about the rat race
Making the world a better place.

What are my favourite things?
The colours lavender and blue
Eating chocolate, going to
The zoo, these are just a few.
Butterflies and ladybirds too
Church bells, pan pipes and music
Writing and receiving a letter
These things always make me feel better.

J Pearson

Ma Foi

A sad farewell Ma Foi
My canine
I had to let you go
Your golden sheen
Those large black eyes
With sadness we had to part
At my feet there you sat
Listening to every sound
With a tilt of your head
You stared at me
Each word you understood
No more to be Ma Foi
The wag of your tail
That greeted me
In you usual friendly way
I thank you Ma Foi
For the time we had
And the pleasure you gave
As I now look back
Upon those years
No more to be, you and I
Goodbye, My Foi.

Marion Gannon

For Someone Special

I get a tingle,
Whenever I see your image there,
The way you talk,
The things you do,
Like how you comb your hair.

Your lovely smell wafts past me,
And lingers in the breeze,
Your childish laugh,
Your blushing cheeks,
Make me tremble at the knees.

Your sweet pink lips,
Remind me of blossom in the spring,
I find now,
I love you,
Is that such a bad thing?

Gareth Davies

RISING DAMP

It started in my toes as cramp -
The human form of *Rising Damp*
In XL jeans I couldn't squeeze
My puffy ankles, chubby knees
The water clogged my thighs and bum
And swished around my bloated tum
My breasts resembled outsized pears
Attracting *most* unwelcome stares . . .
I was pig-sick and *so* shame-faced
To find I measured 40 waist!
Thick sausage fingers on fat palms,
My bulging wrists bore podgy arms
The doctor, seeing head so swollen,
Diagnosed a troubled colon
But it took Gran to make me thin -
She burst me with her safety pin!

Sue Millward

RHYTHMS

Fascinating sounds of rhythm,
From falling rain, to ticking clocks,
Machines, engines, we can hear them,
Their sounds we sometimes try to mock.

The drum is always great to beat,
The skin stretched tight, will rebound sticks,
And drummers perched upon their seats,
Their arms and feet all moving quick.

The single stroke, the buzz roll too,
And solos, they are very grand,
There's such a lot of beats to do,
They'd like to have another hand.

The mamma-dadda of the rolls,
The paradiddles, they sound good,
And marching drummers, just like dolls,
They put us in a happy mood.

The tap dancer, has nimble feet,
With shuffles, time steps, and tap springs,
Can conjure up a special treat,
And create good rhythmical things.

All kinds of wonderful dancers,
Have great rhythmic talent worldwide,
To drums and music, they answer,
They dance with joy, they cannot hide.

To hear all rhythms, is just fine,
It gets within your knowing mind,
Pulsating rhythms of the time,
Has always been there with mankind.

D Ranson

IT'S TIME WE REALISED

Take note you hunters
With trap or gun
To take a life
Is not much fun.

If your family
Were to die
You'd go to pieces
And cry and cry.

So throw away
Your killing things
Study wild life
And the joy it brings.

Shoot with a camera
Instead of a gun
Stand still forever
As they play and run.

Out you go
With your vicious traps
You may not kill
Just hurt perhaps.

So change your mind
They won't hurt you
All they want
Is to live life through.

Please realise
There is more to give
And give all creatures
The right to live.

Brian Stevens

Departure To Oz

When you've flown half round the world
And are hanging upside down.
Think of us poor pommies
With both feet on the ground.
We'll be pounding on the Adlers
Trying to sort out words.
You'll be seeing Koala bears
And more exotic birds.
While you're lapping up the sun
On the palm fringed shores,
We'll be shivering in our boots
Sweeping snow from round the doors.
Suffering more cuts
And taking all the pills
To help our aches and pains
Coughs and colds or chills.
You'll be sipping long cool drinks,
Or nibbling at a peach,
Enjoying Christmas dinner
On some shark infested beach.
So remember all these things
If ever you feel blue,
There may be some of us
Would like to be with you.
But we'll put on Mac's and wellies
To go singing in the rain
The words from that old song -
'Will ye no come back again.'

B Fuller

THE RAINBOW

An experience that I shall never forget
Occurred one gloomy day,
When I was hurrying though the rain
Thinking how dull the day.

But suddenly the sun peeped out
Between those clouds of grey
Bringing a hint of hopefulness
That made me feel quite gay.

It burst in all its glorious light
Forcing the clouds to part,
It changed the scene before my eyes
To one of heavenly art.

It twinkled on the raindrops that
Hung from the leafy trees,
They look like little stars from heaven
When shaken by the breeze.

And then I saw the rainbow arch
Spread right across the sky,
I slowed my hurried footsteps as
I turned to gaze on high.

I thought I heard an angels' choir
Singing triumphantly,
The dazzling colours, blazing bright
So I could hardly see.

The rainbow slowly faded as
I turned to go my way,
But its beauty stayed within my heart
And helped me through the day.

D I Harris

Dashed On Rocks

Wow! What artist has painted such beauty?
What salmon has given its life to streak the
sky with such pink?
What waterfall has danced on silk to parade this
fleeting heaven?
What words can catch the moment, when nature is
in glory?
It's the glittering sea of lights, that truly
insights my intrigue.
In some ways I feel adrift, cast away from the million
moths around flames.
I also, a fragment of light, wonder if I am someone's
ocean.
I begged to be touched, be a part of a wave.
Breaking on hope together, striving to new horizons.
It's true a small fire is greatly hotter, but I wanted
the warmth of a towering inferno.
I wanted in, being different is fine but being the same
is so much easier.
I could swim like the rest, be supported by the current
went weary.
But I felt perpetually beached, marooned from a changing
tide.
Making my own little raft, so one day I'll set sail on
the world.

J Cross

TURKISH SEA

A falling star in a Turkish dawn
made things right for me.
A sail boat rocked with love and laughter
on a turquoise deep blue sea.

A man came there into my mind, my heart
and my body last.
And he smelled of a future that reminded me
of ancient fairy tales from the distant past.

He kissed me awake to sun and rain and snow
until in the end I knew what life was,
praying to God it would always be so.

Now the years of sleep I slept before he came
seem only seconds long, while the moments I
spend awake with him will last my life and beyond.

He says he'll be mine forever now,
well maybe that's not to be.

But if ever I face life or death without him,
my memory will recall, on earth or in heaven,
the falling star in a Turkish dawn that made things right for me.

E Huysinga

MISSED

I'll miss the day I miss you,
I won't care for that day,
I'll miss the day I kiss you,
A passionate display,
And now the missing's ended
I need not care no more,
Now that you've walked out of my life
I've missed you even more.

Will Turner

As Time Goes By

I watch the children playing
laughing merrily
'Pass the ball to me' says one
'Please pass the ball to me.'

Young couples walking hand in hand
Gazing in each other's eyes
What life holds in store for them
Is still one of surprise.

I still remember being young
The dreams I used to share
With my one and only love
For him I truly care.

So even though I'm older
I remember days gone past
Of plans that we both made together
Of memories that last

Sally A Dodsworth

The Garden

It's winter, and it's cold,
The garden is bare, but bold.
A covering of frost
Gives a new dimension,
Everything in suspension.

The warmer air of spring
Puts life into everything,
Suddenly the colour
Begins to show,
Now's the time to grow.

The glory of summer abound,
Just look around.
Feel the warmth of the sun,
Smell the perfume in the air,
Life is fair.

Shades of autumn lower,
Life begins to cower,
Storing up energy
During its hibernation
Ready for the next regeneration.

Ted Baker

The Wheelbarrow

Adam's yoke, with handles smooth and shining,
Cooper's wheel in squeaky need of oiling,
Polished ash, made smoother by the using,
Calloused hands from endless hours of toiling,
Wheelbarrow, trundling to the flower show,
Bearing bigger marrows for the judging.
Village fete, bustle, extravaganza:
Cream teas served on vicarage veranda.

Rusted bolts hold balks of splintered timber,
Planking worn by countless years of labour,
Frames of ash made strong and yet more stronger,
By adze and axe and awl and twisting auger,
Wheeling marrows, drumming over cobbles,
Bigger marrows, better than his rivals',
To the fete and vicious competition,
Prizes for your owner's dedication.

A J Bavin

Between Scenes

When I wake on misty mornings, there's a funny kind of light,
It's as if the sun is still abed, and yet, it's far from night.
I look out of my window, and the world seems so unreal.
The mist drifts through the garden, there's an eerie sort of feel.

It's not *just* the lack of clear sight, that's brought by this low cloud.
When I go out in the garden, things seem muted. Nothing's loud.
It's like we're on a film set. Caught on stage, between the acts.
The scenery's not quite been set. The finished product, something
lacks.
Perhaps God's had a lie in, and I should not be here at all.
That somehow, I've dropped out of time, and should await the
curtain call.
Perhaps, if I go back to bed and close my eyes again.
It will give *Him* time to wave *His* hand, and to make the world
look sane.

Perhaps, *He's* not made up *His* mind, what will occur today.
Perhaps, that great scriptwriter has yet to write the play.
The cast has yet to learn their lines, and to get their act together.
Come on Mr Weatherman! Bring on the brighter weather.

This can't be as it's meant to be. This world of strange phantasm.
Mist drifting all around us, like unearthly ectoplasm.
It's time the show was on the road. Leave this world of no attraction.
Ah! At last! The sun is coming through. Lights up! Run camera!
Action!

R Murphy

QUICK SILVER

I am the sky lark,
I am the crested cockatoo,
I am a sky-bike-cycler of dreams
Whose temperamental hues
Span the rainbow of my spirit
In which life's unpleating fan,
Reflects the butterflies quick,
Silver in my mind.

In the chest of gold dust
That glows behind my eyes,
I plunder with exuberance
Well imaged life experience,
Then jump a starbound trampoline,
And witch wand into summer greens,
The steel edged, knight-ride blue;

Pink cocktails sailed on batwings
Tipped by slipshod djinns,
And pitch black cats with jade green
Eyes, and peacocks in starched trim,
That shrill their courting melodies,
While doves debate their nesting state
And a dolphin sings her song.

Katherine Jane Rawlings

A Moment In Time

One moment in time, one day of the week
Reflections of life, not easy to speak
Everything comes, just as it goes
From this world to the next, no-one really knows.
Treading the path, often uphill,
Reaching for the stars, shining still.
For some life is a battle, that's never quite won
For others, a challenge, that has to be done.
Spanning the years, there's good and there's bad
At the end of the rainbow, be it happy or sad.
Time waits for no man, we have to move on
Making way for newcomers, now our day's work is done.
Somewhere out there, a land waits for us yet
For life is precious, should we forget.

Suzanne Hill

My Grandson

My grandson was born on the 10th of November
A day to remember that day in November.
A precious little bundle of peaches and cream
A beautiful picture like you have never seen.
His little face, his fingers and feet
To look at them was really a treat.
When you hold him in your arms he is so small
The pleasure he gives, nothing else matters at all.
His beautiful eyes are a lovely blue
You just want to melt when he looks at you.
This is how you feel about this little lad
Who is the treasure of his mum and his dad.
As years go by he will be
Someone you will be proud to know.
He is my grandson and his name is Joe.

J B Horsted

Rescue Me

He is my friend, my companion
Fills a big gap in my life
We spend as much time together
As we possibly can
Because that is the way
We both want it to be.
He was abandoned at two years old,
Tied to a rusty old crate
Left to starve in Wales
The song 'We'll Keep A Welcome'
But sadly for him it did not count
Today at the age of four and a bit
He is a cute, happy, healthy little dog
Who is dearly loved by me.
I found him in a dog sanctuary
They had brought him down
Here to the south,
Whoever treated him in this way
Should hang their head in shame
But I am pleased to say
It is their loss and my gain.
To anyone who reads these words
Pause and give thought to my claim,
If you ever suffer a loss of a pet
When you begin to feel better again
Go along to a rescue home.
See for yourself the sadness
The fretting, there is nothing worse
No one likes to feel unwanted
Please give a dog a home.

M Evans

On Meeting Ned

I met this man, he said his name was Ned.
He stopped in his tracks and to me said,
'Can you explain why I feel so spry,'
Then suddenly he sailed up on high.
I grabbed his shoe to try to hold him down,
Then I was flying too in my night-gown.
We flew up into the cold morning air.
And then all the people began to stare.
I really was frightened, I didn't like heights
And wasn't keen to be one of the sights.
People were pointing and showing their friends.
We flew quite high, then began to descend.
A bird nearly hit us as we passed by
And then started to bomb us from up high.
The shock made me lose my hold on Ned's shoe
From that time on I was flying solo too,
But my flight was only on downward trend.
I shuddered to think how my flight would end.
Quickly I tumbled, landing on my head,
Only to find myself there on my bed.
I felt very confused and quite dizzy,
Realised while flying I'd been busy,
I'd been having a realistic dream,
Hadn't even had time to scream.
Ned was a person I had imagined,
I started to laugh but also was saddened,
For when I'd met Ned and he had me charmed,
He'd taught me flying and I'd not been harmed.
I have never more dreamt this dream again
And why I dreamt it then I can't explain.

R Lawrence

The Dawn

I see this light, this gentle creamy
light unfold,
Behind the trees like skeletons
arrayed - with slightly caressing
breeze,
The light gently becomes pure
gold.
Making all the world glow and
the trees like saintly beings -
cold.
But wait - the sunlight wakens
up the earth - warming it,
Even the birds, now become bold.
They sing for joy, of this sweet
happening - as yet untold.

Iris J Hart

Life's Memories

Thoughts come like rays of the setting sun
Shining through memories one by one
First to the time when I was young
And life it seemed hadn't quite begun
And then to my childhood with never a care
On to my teens full of hope and despair
But then Oh joy! To the day I discovered
You and the golden age of lovers

Then came our wedding a wish come true
The years stretched ahead full of love for you
And now growing older it would seem
Life has been a most wonderful dream
If the past and the future could be as one
Then I'll love you the same when life is done.

Doreen Iris Lester

THANKS FOR LIFE

I love baby lambs, I love Mozart and Brahms
I love the beautiful trees,
The children at play on a warm summer's day
I thank God for giving me these,
I love country lanes, and horses with manes
That are plaited to make them look smart,
I love the white snow, that makes my face glow
And makes me feel glad to my heart,
To hear the birds sing, the first day of spring
With flowers of yellow and gold,
My cat's golden eyes, my grandchildren's guys
In November when it's freezing cold
A meal with my friends when our work's at an end
With plenty of fun and laughter,
Then I'll fall into bed, with a prayer in my head
That will linger for ever after
So many things, can make my heart sing,
Bringing peace and joy to me
I thank God above, for sending, down love
And blessings for all to see.

Roma Court

Know That I'm There

When you feel you're alone, with no one to care,
Just think of me and know that I'm there.
If your troubles weigh heavy on life's weary road,
I will always be here, to help share the load.
When you're lost in a turmoil of hurt and dismay,
Ask only of me and I'll show you the way.
Whenever you're scared, afraid to voice any fear,
Talk to me and know that I hear.
When all that you are able to do is cry,
Know I will wipe every tear from your eye.
When you are surrounded by people who do not understand,
Just reach out to me and I'll take your hand.
When you're blinded by lies, place your trust in me
And I will walk with you and help you to see.
Remember that I am always by your side,
Forever your friend, your love and your guide.

Alison James

The Bluebell Glade

Warm zephyrs stirred the glade's soft dappled light,
That filtered down and touched a grazing deer,
Silent I stood to watch with sheer delight,
As perfume filled the air from bluebells near,
That wood was carpeted 'neath every bough,
The doe moved off, sensing someone was there,
Clear in my mind I hold that memory now,
For as a blackbird sang heaven was near.

Barbara Pearton

Hop-Picking

Houses crowd in structured rows -
Urban lives and urban minds;
A modern maze of garden plots
Where once existed different kinds:
Furrows far as eye could see,
The first acknowledged glimpse of green,
Cat's-cradle strings from pole to pole,
A haze of foliage in between;
And in September's mellow sun,
Pickers came from far and near,
Families clad in oldest clothes -
The highlight of their working year;
And then the early day began:
A mighty pull, the bines collapse
Around the rotund basket's side,
Pungent cones on copious laps,
Then weathered fingers deftly slide
And mount the harvest to the brim.
Brown limbed children help or hinder,
Till the shortening day grows dim.
A time of close camaraderie,
Anticipation of the pay,
Then with fingers stained and sticky,
Home, before another day.

I Coventry

Rekindled Romance

It's a hot sunny day,
  I need to get away.
Some time to unwind,
  A break from the daily grind.
A few days by the coast,
  That's what I'd like most,
To walk on the sand,
  Have someone hold my hand.
Feel the sea breeze on my face,
  A time for embrace.
Hear the gulls overhead,
  Passionate word softly said.
Run into the sea,
  Feeling carefree.
Taste the salt on my lips,
  Feel the waves reach my hips.
Come alive and be free,
Have some time to be me.
Annual leave I am due,
  So out of the blue.
I booked up the break
  In a cottage, by a lake.
A second honeymoon, I'd hoped it would be,
  Rekindled romance, I wanted to see.
A sandy beach was nearly,
  My dream I'll see before I die.
Well, our fantasy came true,
  And 'Yes,' my darling, 'I still love you.'

Hazel McCluskey

Time Runs Ever Faster

A Saxon King, buried in his proud ship, armour burnished bright
In a few short years, nothing to show where earthly power lies,
no body skeletal, only useless gold is left where once the king was laid.
Statues carved in later ages, glorifying saints or famous men
standing on plinths or abbey porches, scoured by time worn faceless by the wind
Inside our sepulchres of death, battered faces lie on tombs
memorial brasses polished smooth, telling nought of those beneath, reflecting only light of moon.
'Neath churchyard grass, a charnel house of bones, no smart burial suits survive
no silks or satin pillows, no night clothes thin, headstones smashed or levelled, silent is life's din.
What things we do - that we are not forgotten, painted faces lifted breasts
to chase away the hurrying curse of age, life passes quickly
like a swift turned page.
Yet desperately we fight to drive away the ravages of time
etched year by year upon our faces - in ever deeper lines.

Howard W Gibbs

Young Excavators

They pull on gumboots, raise three hoods
    And charge into the field,
When low skies strike and wind spears thrust
    The duffel gives a shield.

Where furrowed soil heaps claybound lumps
    They search for treasure lost,
On humble kitchen's hard cold floor
    The fragments hedge-high tossed.

Each earthworn piece is basket placed
And kitchen borne once more,
To greet again the sud warm sink
Above that gravestone floor.

Each pattern softly coloured still
Is lit with pleased surprise,
And finds new life in jagged death
Made whole through children's eyes.

Jean Young

MY KINDLED SPIRIT

Never will I kindle the fire
That flames within my heart,
For it's the spirit of my Lord
He is inside taking part,
In weary ways where heavy shadows be,
He knoweth best and leadeth me,
And may my longing for Him be never stilled,
My mission for Him must be fulfilled,
His love ordains me pleasant things
Source of life, refreshing springs,
Under his shadow I safely lie,
While dreaded evils pass me by,
At times when I can see no way,
Let me trust and still obey,
My kindled fire will never loose its flame,
And forever I'll sing praises to His name.

Marion Staddon

The Attic

The attic holds the memories
Of those many golden years
The boxes tied with ribbons
Holding happiness and tears

The tennis racquets old and worn
Show several broken strings
Reminds us of how we played
It's as though the years have wings

The letters and the books are there
With toys that you've left behind
The train track spreads the floorboards
Space so difficult to find

You've grown up now and left us
Time to sort the attic through
But I hear dad in the loft
Calling 'This is Waterloo'

As we dream amongst the treasures
That we cannot give away
We try to stop a sunset
At the closing of the day.

Marian Acres

A Grandparent's Treasure

Peak cap set jauntily
On pony-tailed fair hair,
Eyes light blue and sparkling
From an open face without a care.

Wearing knee-holed blue jeans
Over a creased denim shirt
To which many badges are pinned,
Football team heroes preferred.

This is a child whose sweet way of giving
Fills a grandparent's heart with the true joy of living,
The love and affection is especially treasured
Bringing joy and blessings too great to be measured.

Who is this treasure
A girl or a boy?
It's our grand-daughter, Emma
A cherished tom-boy!

Florence Scott

For A Son

Come little one, come with me
There are wonderful things to see
Bubbling, running, laughing streams
Fish, and flowers. Golden dreams
New mown hay, shady trees
Long summer days, gentle breeze
Yellow waving fields of corn
Leaping lambs newly born.
See the baby rabbits run
Grass snakes basking in the sun
Overhead the skylark sings
A hovering hawk on silent wings
May you recall with wondrous joy
The secret world of a little boy
As nature's gifts in your heart you store
Remember your childhood evermore.

Hazel M Hann

On Holiday

You cannot measure a summer in yellow-hammers.
With their slightly fuzzy sound of warmth and well-being
They linger over into autumn:
Summer is shorter than that -
We need something sharper.
What is there to define
Rare hours of sunshine
As you lie under a cliff, legs perhaps crossed,
But the grass-hopper calling?
I know nothing braver:
A wet season's waiting
For the right time to sing -
If it can be called singing.
It is rarer than that even -
A controlled virtuosity of impossibilities,
A noise thrown off with insouciance
And then finished
As the cloud comes again.
Bizarre limbs evolved for bizarrer purposes,
Patience, skill and tact,
A sense of the dramatic
('This may not happen again till next year!')
The right moment of sun
And this holiday-maker is at it,
His recognition clicking in your ear
And then done.

Alasdair Aston

Gone Are The Days

Gone are the days,
When she ran with glee,
On feet so small
A joy to see.

Gone are the days.
With blonde hair flying,
She ran to and fro,
With sharp eyes spying.

Gone are the days,
When she said 'I can do it'
Her little hands covered with soap.
She just knew it.

Gone are the days,
When her little arms,
Would curl 'round our necks,
With such wonderful charm.

Gone are the days.
When she was so small,
This little girl,
Has grown so tall.

A teenager now,
With lots to do,
No time to say,
Mum and dad, 'I love you.'

Muriel Bowles

Isle Of Purbeck

Throughout the seasons of the year,
I've come to this sweet Dorset place,
Whose constant beauty I hold dear . . .
Like the features of a much loved face.

Today I'm treading the shifting sand,
And the hills of Purbeck beckon as before,
Mysterious and beautiful . . . this my promised-land
Even in winter I bow to your allure.

February's chilly smile . . .
And the wind blowing . . .
Shells and seaweed . . . flight of birds,
Send my feet moving like water flowing,
As once again the young year stirs.

Razor shells strewn on the ridged sands,
And straggled seaweed's pungent smell . . .
Coarse grasses swaying on the dunes,
A Truckline nosing through the swell.

Skimming the winter waves . . . flying low,
The flock of oyster-catchers wheel into shore . . .
A study in black and white the sea-birds go,
Searching for food along the sandy floor.

Spindly pink legs running swiftly along . . .
Red bills poised . . . and bright eyes flicker,
I hear the high-pitched whistle of their song . . .
Even the breeze moves scarcely quicker!

Flying in groups . . . with showy displays
Of black and white tails and wings . . .
A chattering throng flitting down the days . . .
A part of the lovely, abiding things.

Isle of Purbeck . . . close to the restless sea . . .
I watch the wintry sun sink in the West,
And your timeless enchantment captures me . . .
I'm happy once more to have been your guest.

Noni Fanger

THROUGH FIELDS OF GREEN

Through fields of green I wander
down to a running stream. Where
I sit and watch the sunrise
in a place that's so serene.

Just to sit here in the morning
light. So peaceful and at ease
and listen to the silence and
feel the gentle breeze.

But then the world awakens and
the birds begin to sing. The
land has come alive with
every living thing.

So when the day is over and
the sun lays down to rest and
the land once more is silent
then the world is at its best.

But I will be back tomorrow
through my fields so green
and watch another sunrise
in my place that's so serene.

E Hiddleston

Mr Henry

My Henry has been smoking since he was a boy of eight.
Mr Henry's fifty-nine, meditating, the morning cold air
blows upon his naked body,
while smoke balloons his lungs.

Mabel empties studded ashtrays,
opening windows for a gasping room.
Leaving a feast, Mr Henry
smokes between the courses.
Leaving the theatre thankfully,
he puffs in the passage
until the next act.

The groove in the lower lip
eagerly awaits his next cigarette
he eats morsels and no longing
for stimulating cups of tea.
Smoking is sufficient
unto the day. Hesitating
before lighting another -
momentarily.

Mr Henry lives for smoking
and will die as he has lived.

Angela Brennan

My Map Is Crumpled

You spoke with such assurance when I asked
'Should we talk it through?'
'No need' you said,
'We're well on the road.'
But which road? And where does it lead from here?
No lines link where my eyes search,
Rock shapes jag up from the bunched page since that day:
My map is crumpled.

Perhaps I will draw my own new, smooth, perfect, personal map,
My carte blanche,
But it would be so separate.
You don't even recognise I am on a path
When I walk beside you.

Daphne Rance

Who's Disabled?

One times two is two
Two times two is four
Someone kind to care for me
I ask for nothing more
To speak I am unable
To move I am unsure
You'd think I was an object
to be shoved behind the door
Don't look at me with pity
Don't clothe me in your shame
It's my life you're holding
not a child's game
Although outside I'm stupid
Inside I'm really bright
But because I cannot tell you
I've lost the will to fight
So next time that you see me
As I stumble on my way
Remember that I'm human
And don't just turn away.

D McMillan

SOUP OF THE DAY

Filigree-laced, delicate hue
Make this an interesting
Ingredient to choose.

Crepe de chine texture,
Sand washed silk
Blending sensuality
To a melt-in-the-mouth smoothness.

An aroma unmatched wafts
Through the air
Leaving the recipient
On tender hooks
In mouth-watering anticipation
Of an experience
So delightfully unique
The buds of taste
Become weak at the knees,
Trembling with lust
For the pure pleasure
Of mushroom soup.

Beverley Beck

WHAT SHALL I DO?

What shall I do about you?
If I asked a friend
They'd say it's not true,
That no-one could feel the way that I do,
O, what shall I do about you?

What should I do with your smile?
When thinking about it
Time and awhile,
It sets my heart racing mile after mile
O, what should I do with your smile?

What should I do with your kiss?
For there's nothing at all
That I would more miss,
In memories of you the first would be this
O, what shall I do with your kiss?

And what should I do with your love?
If I were without it
Heavens above!
I am the hand and you are the glove,
O, what shall I do with your love?

V Evans

JANINE

You never saw the light of day
before your life was taken away,
And you never had the chance to see,
the faces of your mother and me.
You didn't ask to be conceived, yet
your arrival it was ill-received.
Had I been a stronger man, you
would have become part of life's great plan.
But I have to confess that I was
weak, and the easy option I did seek.
I let your mother terminate, the
pregnancy I did germinate.
I hope in heaven you will understand,
that your arrival was never planned.
But on earth is a mum and dad,
who'll always remember the girl they never had.
Your mum and I are far apart,
but she is always in my heart.
So when in heaven we all do meet,
our family once more will be complete.

David Paginton

REVIVAL

The dreary days of winter
Now firmly out of sight
The first sign of springtime
Snowdrops snowy white
Sap surges through bush and treetops
Buds turn to leafy green
Earth stirs with gentle movement
New growth will soon be seen
Birds trill out their lovesongs
Calling for a mate
To start again the nestings
That nature doth dictate
Drifting clouds and sunshine
Showers of gentle rain
Fills hearts with the joy of living
And revival once again
Beautiful flowers - good food to eat
From labours of love remaking
The wonders of the natural world
Are ours just for the taking.

A Cutler

THE LIGHT

The wonder of the sunshine
That once I could only feel,
The dawning of the daylight,
After darkness, is it real?

An abundance of flowers
With their colours so gay,
I could gaze by the hour
And with joy, I would pray.

May the glories of my garden
The trees, the birds and bees,
The wind gently begging its pardon
As I'm down upon my knees.

Let me keep this joy forever
With my world of darkness gone,
The light of life, my pleasure
But 'blind' memories will linger on.

Isabel Temperley

The Cornfield

Cast your mind to lovely summer days
To where the corn grows and gently sways
As a golden carpet rippling in the gentle breeze
Growth has ended, standing mature, leisurely at ease
Awaiting the harvest under the warmth of long sunny days
Where time stands still, at peace, lost in a haze
Soon will come the reapers when the hush will be disturbed
By the hum of the harvesters, cutting
Steadily beating, thrashing the grain
Leaving behind the stubble to be gently washed
And bathed by summer's gentle rain
Poppies had grown around the edge
Creating a patterned border
Finally to be cut down to order
Lying as droplets of blood rich and red
Depicting knives cause lifeblood to be shed
There scurries the fieldmouse escaping the blades
That life may continue in other surrounding glades.

Evelyn A Evans

KARAOKE

The smoke-filled room is full of noise
With mums and dads and girls and boys
My palms are wet I wait in fear
For soon it's my turn to appear
As each one sings, applause rings out
My time will come, there is no doubt
With trembling knees and shaking hands
We all perform to well-known bands
The moment's come, my heart beats loud
But no-one hears in this great crowd
I walk onto the stage so high
and silence falls, there's not a sigh
My hand it grasps the 'mic' so cold
I stand transfixed, as in a mould
The music starts and I breathe deep
My voice rings out and I could weep
It sounds so rich and full to me
My trembling stops, I'm full of glee
The audience stares, there's not a sound
Only music and my voice resound
and as the last note of my song
Dies away in silence long
I wait and suddenly to my ears
Tumultuous clapping stops my fears
I've done it and I'm on a high
I bow and smile and I could fly
This was the first time but I know
It's not the last, I loved it so.

Edwina Fooks

Berkshire Downs

We love the good old Berkshire Downs,
My wife, my dog, and I;
So far away from busy towns,
Too dull, too hot, too dry;
With gentle breeze when sun is strong,
To guide us as we stroll along,
In rhythm with the skylark's song,
This is the place where we belong,
My wife, my dog, and I.

We love the downland air so clear,
My wife, my dog, and I;
Far from polluted atmosphere,
No fume, no smell, no fly;
To feel the downland carpet's spring,
And watch the harebells dance and swing,
As though they hear the fairies sing,
We feel as proud as any king,
My wife, my dog, and I.

We often rest in beechwood shade,
My wife, my dog, and I;
So far away from things man-made,
No house, no barn, no sty;
Beside those trees with leaves bright green,
Where birds are heard but seldom seen,
Just for a while we too have been,
Part of a picture so serene,
My wife, my dog, and I.

David Leonard Taylor

My Mother's Blue Eyed Boys

When I told my three brothers
Bob was marrying me,
They all danced about with glee
'We will toss for who sleeps
In her vacant bedroom
When are you getting married - soon?'

The eldest one said
'It is my point of view
You could call this
The taming, of the shrew'

The second one said
'Bob must be mad
But I'll give him a medal
He's a very brave lad'

The youngest one said
'This settles for me
The problem of presents
He'll get my sympathy

If father is ill
On her wedding day
We are all volunteering
To give her away'

Ann Saxty

KENT IS MY COUNTY

Kent is my county
Kent my birth home
You're always a base
Wherever I roam

A county of beauty
There's none to compare
Which is probably why
Everyone moves there

Spring is blossoms
Covering the trees
Summer is strawberry
picking, on your knees

Autumn a time
For fruit and hops
Roads lined with tractors
That almost never stop

In winter the Downs
Covered in snow
Kent the most beautiful
County I know

R A Quinney

Changes

I knew from the start,
it would not be easy.
From shelter of abbey,
to red-brick church.
It was a challenge,
a new beginning for me.
The people I knew,
were watching me close.
The old vicar, they had
hated to let go, but he
had moved on six months ago,
now it was up to me.
So one year later,
I thought I had made it.
But tonight I was shocked,
by a hostile silence,
when I invited the
newcomers to read, at
a celebration of our
risen Lord, who died
to save us all.
There's a world out there,
you cannot shut it out.
So open the doors, let
the people in, into the
church, into our hearts.
Be not afraid of change,
with love in our hearts,
and God on our side.
Together we will survive!

Audrey Allen

FOOD FOR THOUGHT

Now what can we have for dinner today?
Something just for a change.
With four fussy children to feed
It's quite hard to arrange.

We could have toad in the hole I suppose,
But Ryan doesn't like toads,
And I haven't got any holes left either,
So that idea explodes.

Oh, I know, we could have shepherd's pie,
I think that would suit them all,
But no, the Co-op's sold out of shepherds,
And anyway the oven's too small.

Welsh rarebit sounds a good idea,
But Peter's allergic to cheese,
Perhaps if I look at the cookery book
I might find something to please.

Fish fingers might be an option,
But Michele and Dave won't eat those,
I didn't know fish had any fingers,
Wonder if they've got any toes?

Well I don't know what to give them,
I can't change the menu it seems,
If I want to keep them all happy,
It will just have to be chips and beans!

Carol Carroll

Life's Stages

Life comes in stages first we are born
As we lay in our cot on that first ever morn
The world is a wonder a joy to behold
To our mother and father we are as precious as gold
As we grow and we learn along life's rocky path
We can walk and run and communicate fast
Now we're at playgroup and making new friends
Learning new skills we can use until the end
The school gates are beckoning there's learning to do
Reading and writing and everything new
A teenager next with a future to build
Studying first for a City and Guild
Next come relationships varied and mixed
We're up and we're down sometimes getting hitched
So wedding bells chime a new start once more
Maybe it will work we don't know what's in store
A family of our own now God's wonderful gift
Whatever our problems now soon take a lift
As our family grows grandparents we become
Our life now seems to go at a very fast run
The aches and the pains come in one by one
And we often look back at the things we have done
That's all we have now, we live from day to day
Not knowing when we'll be called away
So a life full of pleasure also of pain
We've lived in the sunshine and also the rain
As long as we've made the best of our lot
No more can we ask when we reach a full stop

Rosalyn English

New Babe

Hour of birth, new babe arrives
Nine months in womb survived
Into this dangerous world leap
Noisy world where none can sleep
Helpless, quite naked, yell that's loud
Mum and dad seem very proud.

New babe's birthday, this day two
Learn to crawl, needs no shoes
Use his knees scuffs the ground
Now has found new way round
Shoes on wrong, left on right
Holds table tightly to keep upright.

Shoes that's strong, great world walk
Chatters all day, learnt to talk
Mum in tears, vanished, now gone
Did not leave babe alone long
Hands in everything he can find
Quiet under table, knitting to unwind.

Time it slips, years they slide
Time to face this world wide
A million miles must walk alone
Into a man now has grown
Build his home, his future meet
Face great world on own feet.

P Powell

Our Garden

The garden's a place of wonder to me
Brings forth such life a pleasure to see.
Seasons come and seasons go
And in turn each one I know.

Leaves of autumn fall to the ground
Rich in colour they are to be found.
Piled upon the compost heap
Left awhile for a little sleep.

Bleakness of winter a preparation
Just resting a time for rejuvenation.
Sparrows and starlings they want to be fed
Wild birds so hungry, the winter they dread.

Spring and the garden awakens
Crocus and snowdrops, of these there are oceans.
Iris and daffodils a beautiful display
Tulips and violas, they'll be gone by May.

Summer and the garden's alive
Abundance of colour, flowers Oh how they strive!
Long hours of sunshine during the day
Lightness now for a while will stay.

N A Taylor

My Epitaph

Don't mourn for me when I've passed away
Just read my poetry that's here to stay
Help the poor animals suffering in pain
And think of the homeless out in the rain

Think of the poor old pensioners
Whose lives are so bleak
They don't get enough money
To help them with their heat

The good people out there
Who have the money
Please help them to live
Put your hand in your pocket
And be a good Christian and give

You find you get a good feeling in giving
Because you know you are helping the living
All the ones you are helping are saying a prayer
For the ones that are doing the giving

I'd like to thank the ones that were giving
The title says I'm not one of the living
One day in heaven I will join up with them
And I will hold out my hand
And say thank you dear friend.

Bert Booley

Gemma

I looked, and saw such sad eyes
As she lay upon that floor,
She lifted her head so slowly
Please, she seemed to say, no more.

I spoke, so softly she hardly heard
'Come to me I really care,'
She lifted her head so slowly
And she wondered if she dare.

I'd heard, the foot and fist she knew
No one to fuss or pat,
She lifted her head so slowly
So I sat down on the mat.

I waited, and she came to look
And laid down beside me,
She lifted her head so slowly
And seemed to say 'Please guard me.'

I decided, she should be my own
I knew that she would come,
She joyfully looked up to say
She knew she had come home.

I'm happy, she is happy too
And now she knows no fear,
She lifts her head so slowly
And she knows she is so dear.

I rescued her, from fear and pain
And now she's clean and fed,
She lifts her head so slowly
From her warm and comfy bed.

Patricia Gray

Have You Ever?

Have you ever climbed a mountain
Right up to the top,
Then run right down the other side
And thought you'd never stop?

Have you ever raced along the shore,
Right after the morning tide,
Your footprints first upon the sand,
Increasing with each stride?

Have you ever sunbathed in the snow,
Shivered on burning sands?
Have you ever kissed a pretty girl,
Without first shaking hands?

Can you say 'do' instead of 'don't'?
Instead of 'won't' say 'will'?
Then for you the mountain high
Is just a small molehill.

If all these things you may have done,
And you can swear they're true,
Then you're so much in love with life
And life's in love with you.

Can you greet the dawn without a yawn?
The daybreak with a smile?
Just say 'Hello' as you pass folks by
And make their life worthwhile?

The moral of this story,
Yes, it has a tale to tell,
The wondrous things in life are free,
Like water from a well.

J Freeman

RECOLLECTIONS

How thick the beech trees grew
A bluebell wood and cowslips too
        Weston Hills
        Toboggan spills
Picnics in September
        Remember?
Garden parties at the house of the Dean,
Standing on corners to glimpse the Queen.
Tennis played at old Heath Hall,
Tell me really do you recall?

'Yes my darling,' she would say
As you chose your fruit on market day
With rosy cheeks and a happy smile
It made your shopping really worthwhile.
        Remember?
Often we queued for bread and snacks
And a racing tip we got a Jack's
'Twas here we met the folks we knew,
Maybe, one of them could have been you.
        Remember?
The rector visited on his motorbike,
The bells pealed tunes on Midsummer night.
The fair in October was a special treat
Where boy and girl would often meet.
        Remember?
The town has its memories more than a few
Yes of Roman days, Dick Turpin too.
        Baldock is proud
And so are you
        To remember.

Joan Brazier

UP IN THE ATTIC

Where is it, what I'm looking for?
I know I still have it that's for sure.
Where can it be? I know it's around somewhere,
Maybe in the attic, somewhere up there.
I find the step ladders and the lamps,
Cor it's quite chilly and a bit damp.
Gosh where do I start?
It would be spooky if it were dark.
I see a picture of a child with a ball,
Used to hang on the bedroom wall.
The baby's highchair and a cot,
A cardboard box with old birthday cards.
Getting rid of them will be hard,
Must get and clean up this mess.
I really will do my best.
Some paperwork and blankets too,
With a put-up bed, a mattress in blue,
A child chair with table to match.
How on earth did we get this up the hatch?
Well what have I here, my hockey stick,
And my old games kit.
School books and black and white TV.
These have brought back memories to me.
Now I've been here for hours on end,
Mostly sorted out, some to the junk yard I'll send,
Some was fun, it was not a bore,
Now what was it I was looking for?

Christine Kowalkowski

Rollerblading In The Park (A Craze In 1995)

They swarmed into the pathways
of Hyde Park, by Rotten Row
and round by the Serpentine,
racing, bending, swaying and
twisting like a whirlwind.

Four wheels lengthways on a blade
built into knee-high boots,
helmet, knee and elbow caps
is the gear; as they rolled
up and down, and wheeled around;
'They are maniacs, bar them from
the park,' a woman shouted
as she scurried from their path.

I envied them their swiftness,
their limber limbs, their nerve,
no fear of falls or fractures,
excitement glowing their faces;
as I dozed in my deck chair
the years like those wheels rolled back
and I went rollerblading.

Abina Russell

Knickers In A Twist

I've never met a person yet,
Who enjoys a trip to the launderette.
Waiting around to grab a machine,
Hoping they've left it fairly clean.
Somewhere in all the suds and mist,
Your knickers are getting in a rare old twist.
They just keep turning round and round,
To a dull, boring, moaning sound.
It turns to the left, then to the right,
There is something dark amongst the light.
Now it's stopped to have a break,
How much longer will it take?
Hang on it's revving up to go
Practising a touch of quick, quick, slow.
It's getting itself in a right old spin.
Twenty machines dancing a synchronised din.
Finished at last, 30 seconds more.
Then you open that programmed door.
Your washing now smells nice and clean.
God bless the inventor of the washing machine.

J G Vicente

NEW LIFE SPRINGS

Don't rush along hurrying so fast wherever you are going,
Take a little time to see and feel the changes that are showing.
Take time to see and appreciate the beauty of nature's way,
Miraculous workings all around us, new happenings each day.

The more you look,
The more you'll feel the fresh new life that's growing,
And as the hours and days go by
There's a little more newness showing.
Plants are waking from their winter sleep,
And brown earth is looking greener,
While happy playful chirpy birds are singing songs much keener.

The mornings are much brighter now,
And evenings stay lighter longer too,
In the sky fluffy, thinner clouds mean the sun can shine right through.
The wind that has been blowing so cold,
Now brings a fresh new feeling,
New life springs up all around, winter's brutal scars are healing.

After the bitter cold of winter with its damp dark dreary days,
A brand new start, sweet new life, and brighter cheery ways.
So as you're walking here and there, wherever you are bound,
Why not take a little more time to enjoy the changes all around.

J Bilyard

The Rush-Hour Race

It's five o'clock, we've finished work, come on let's go.
The rush-hour race is on, feel the adrenaline flow.
Workers, like ants, converge at the stairs
That lead to the subway. Who's pushing? Who cares?
Hardened commuters with a programmed route,
Shoppers and day-trippers falter, who gives a hoot?
The battle drum beat of the ticket barriers
Urges us forward and like ancient warriors
We advance on the escalators and launch ourselves down.
Only one thing matters, to get out of town.

The platform is seething, a train must be due,
But we must find the right spot, we must get through.
As the train draws near a hot wind precedes it,
We have almost reached our place and at the last minute
We push to the front to be the first on,
Those getting off are slow. Come on, come on!
At last we squeeze in and grab hold a rail,
It's hot and it's sweaty, the air smells stale.
We survive by not moving and taking short breaths,
This ordeal could easily cause early deaths.

We finally arrive at our destination
But the race starts again towards the train station.
It's all in reverse but it's just as frenetic,
We have to keep moving, the train's in, quick, quick!
We jump in the last car as the whistle is blown,
There are seats! Oh bliss, we collapse with a moan.
Now just half an hour and we're nearly there,
There's only the bus ride or a taxi to share.
We start to wind down, the evening beckons,
And tomorrow we'll try to knock off a few seconds!

Pauline Mills

THE TESTING TIMES

The days pass and distance the sorrow
By what means can we make time borrow?
Finding our everydays with stress and tears
Always we make our less seem our worse fears

Forgetting the flooding gates
For where some take refuge
It's the same for the few
Who search for the road
And pay their dues

Our instincts we fail to resist
Completing our routines in which others assist
A failing life in limbo led
This life we've failed the contest
A contest into which wasn't read

Options, advice, no spiritual plantation
Where does the nourishment come from to succeed?

From finding yourselves within be patient
Don't fall prey to false idolatry
Read, listen, seek and knock
Blessed you'll be as firm as a rock.

Clive Bell

The Day We Said Goodbye

(Dedicated to Dean Crawley, the man who changed my life and stole my heart)

I've reached a big decision,
But one that made me cry,
To let us go our separate ways,
And for us both to say goodbye.

The pain I feel, increases,
As every day goes by,
And from time to time, I know I will,
Keep asking myself why?

You see you meant the world to me,
And now we are no more,
And occasionally I have wondered how,
I survived, alone, before.

Please know this, that I could never,
Forget the times we shared,
And the thing inside that keeps me going,
Is the fact that you had cared.

So without each other we will go on,
Many times I'll break down and cry,
When I sit alone and remember well
The day we said goodbye.

Maria Cracknell

West Highland Wet

The steel grey wind-churned water
Frets with wild waves the cooling land,
As wind-blown lochs
And tide-sucked grasses
Tear at the pebbles
On the flotsam strand.

No sunshine lights the grey glen rocks
Beside the rivers swollen after rain;
The brackened outcrops
With their fronded slopes
Fade into sepia
Through the mists again.

Bedraggled hapless sheep are huddled close,
And Keppoch's fields beneath the leaden sky
Sag with the sodden
Humps of Keppoch bog
That squelch and ooze in hollows
Where deep puddles lie.

The sands of Morar do not sing today,
Nor do birds sing amongst her circling trees;
Her blackberries unripened
Line forsaken lanes,
Her driftwood shores as desolate
As her darkening seas.

At Mallaig grey gulls hover by the boats
Whose nets and tackle string the harbour wall -
Only the ferry
Braves the gale force winds
Weaving its zigzag course
Across to Armadale.

Eileen King

Books

All my life I've read in books
Of dashing heroes and wicked crooks
Suspects who tell misleading lies
Astronauts and foreign spies
Of magic islands and mystic spells
A cave wherein a monster dwells
Of kings and queens and maidens fair
Or discovering something very rare
A sword fight with a final thrust
And a wicked enemy bites the dust
A rich heiress in pensive muse
Sailing away on an ocean cruise
Exotic islands in the sun
Where everyone is having fun
Of chivalry and knights so bold
And now that I am growing old
I long to have adventures too
Experiences which are entirely new
To travel to some far-off shore
Find hidden treasure beneath a floor
In some old ruin, when I was lost
or in a boat to be storm-tossed
Saved by helicopter from the cruel sea
Alas nothing like that ever happened to me
So I live my dreams in each new novel
Where the wicked are always made to grovel
The handsome hero wins at last
And trouble fades into the past
If it wasn't for the library
How dull and boring life would be.

J A Sida

Caring Love

This cosy, glowing feeling,
Of comfort with no pain,
Has replaced my sorrow,
Not to come back again.
You couldn't stop for long,
You didn't stay for tea;
But still you knocked my door,
And came to visit me.
Your warm and gentle being,
Your tender loving kiss,
Your caring arms around me,
They filled my heart with bliss.
They showed me that you love me,
And told me that you care;
You didn't have to tell me,
It showed 'cos you were there.
These moments in your arms,
Will last my whole life through;
I know that I'm a dreamer,
But this dream did come true.

Valerie Smith

Cloud

Dispersing and assembling cloud,
High mountains ever-changing shroud.
Dark islands in a still evening sky,
Over whose shores winged squadrons fly,
Uninhabited, doomed to disappear
As blackest night draws near.
Or broken by a sudden breeze, blown on
To find another place to shower upon.
Maybe glide to meet a larger form,
Thus becoming fierce in raging storm.
Oh clouds, how plain the azure blue,
if the heavens were forever without you.
How dull the sunset with no pink frills,
Just a fiery ball behind the hills.
Moisturous mass, not always stayed,
Maker of floods, giver of shade.
Dispersing and assembling cloud,
High mountains ever-changing shroud.

Dorothy French

THE FAIRY GRANDMOTHER

She has family in the USA.
Son distant, imprecise and kindly
Now divorced from the mother of his children.
Gangling grandsons and a lovely grand-daughter
Who spend the long summers here
Walking in the sun, lounging on the beach
Leading swimming into the turbulent Solent
In a heat haze of getting acquainted.
She has all our blood in her veins
A fierce, grumpy grandma to cry over
The family gather around her
The weather-beaten face lights up to a smile
Listen to the good fairy who settles all disputes.
Pubs carry our family name, in Ireland
She tells her in a postcard,
About time they named a street after you here.

Marie K Rooney

SCOTLAND

Oh we're off to bonny Scotland, we leave on Sunday morn
to the land of lochs and castles, where Robbie Burns was born
we'll sit there eating porridge, made from natural oats
they reckon that will fill us up from Fife to John O'Groats
we'll buy ourselves a haggis, and cut the thing in two
'Here's a bit for me' I'll say, and 'here's a bit for you'
we'll sit there by the loch, trying not to make a mess
and if we do not like it we'll throw it in for *Ness*
we'll visit a distillery and have a laugh and sing
and after all those whiskies, we'll do the highland fling
we'll book into a castle with a big four-poster bed
the one they say is haunted by a lady with no head
The land of pipes and tartan kilts (where nothing under's worn)
Oh we're off to bonny Scotland where Robbie Burns was born.

Gayle Moitié Brookes

JUST A THOUGHT ON 7TH SEPTEMBER 1996

Suddenly the years have passed away
I'm living now from day to day
Thinking about what I could have done
Travelling through countries following the sun
Eating gourmet meals in restaurants at night
Wearing latest fashions, looking quite a fright
Flying very high in a colourful balloon
I could have been an astronaut visiting the moon
Discovered new planets studying the sky at night
Rescuing fellow citizens observing their plight
Taken the stage in theatre; studied opera's exciting score
Been a David Attenborough; who could ask for more
Entered the arenas at Hickstead jumping high
Been a professional golfer parring the world as I passed by
All these exciting things I've missed. Why Oh why was this
I was busy being a mother; being hugged and loved and kissed.

Marjorie Gwynn

A DAY AT THE RACES

Field-glass eyes in weatherbeaten stands,
air gently wafting from distant ice-cream van.
Kaleidoscope colours against velvet green.
Flouncing ladies and floppy-brimmed hats,
young pin-striped gentlemen real cool cats.
Champagne corks in jubilant toasts,
jellied eel and king prawn picnic hosts.
White glove tic-tacs scarecrowing air,
black limousines with gleaming stares.
Jockey silks of epaulette and braid,
fiery chestnut thoroughbreds on parade.
Children's dodgem and carousel dreams,
Madame Shilling's day and night fashion theme.
Cheers exploding against the sky.

P Dunne

GOING AWAY

This is a very simple card to say
I know you are going away.

But you are not going away to stay
Because God would not have it that way.

You are going away just for a short stay
God would guide you all the way

God would give you the power to survive
Because He knows what you're leaving behind.

So when the time comes for you to leave
We your children would not have to grieve.

All we have to do is to get on our knees
And pray and God would send you back
To us in the safest way.

T Daniels

Birthmark!

Small country church; square shaped tower;
Single handed clock, calibrating the hour.
Entrance; old tithe gate;
Thing of past, relative to date.
Tomb and gravestones, in the fore;
Century aged, maybe more!
Pretty little posy; large bunched flower;
Indicated thoughts of loved ones, hadn't gone sour!
Stone wall and railing, enveloped the surround;
Peace in store; seemingly bound!
Upon, inscription plate; sheltered by, alcove door;
Names of those fallen, the first world war!
This place, many years ago;
When as a child, I'd come to know!
A memory, from my past;
Looking down, at Bess (my dog), murmured;
'Home at last'.

Robert Denham

GERIATRIC

Old George's eyes were dim
as he sat in his wheelchair.
He could only sit and stare.
'He's a poet
and don't know it,'
someone giggled. 'No chance of a verse
today.'
'He's getting worse!'
(His wife's dismay.)
She recited reams
about woods, pebbled streams,
fields of lusty corn.
She read from George's book
revealing all their dreams.
'Your poems are so beautiful,' I said.
Old George threw me a look.
For one magic moment he nodded his head.

Peggy Trott

INFORMATION

We hope you have enjoyed reading this book - and that you will continue to enjoy it in the coming years.

If you like reading and writing poetry drop us a line, or give us a call, and we'll send you a free information pack.

Write to :-

Arrival Press Information
1-2 Wainman Road
Woodston
Peterborough
PE2 7BU
(01733) 230762